WILLPOWER

IT'S NOT WHAT YOU'VE BEEN THROUGH, BUT IT'S HOW YOU GET THROUGH

WILLPOWER

IT'S NOT WHAT YOU'VE BEEN THROUGH, BUT IT'S HOW YOU GET THROUGH

WILLIAM (KEEPS) HOLMES

WITH DANNY BEYER

BookPress® publishing

While this is a work of non-fiction based on the author's life, many of the names within this book have been changed to protect individual privacy.

Published in Des Moines, Iowa, by:
Bookpress Publishing
P.O. Box 71532
Des Moines, IA 50325
www.BookpressPublishing.com

Publisher's Cataloging-in-Publication Data

Names: Holmes, William, 1973- , author. | Beyer, Danny, author.
Title: WillPower : it's not what you've been through , but it's how you get through / by Will (Keeps) Holmes; with Danny Beyer.
Description: Des Moines, IA: Bookpress Publishing, 2023.
Identifiers: LCCN: 2023936809 | ISBN: 9781947305779 (hardcover) | 9781947305885 (paperback)
Subjects: LCSH Holmes, Will. | Musicians--Biography. | Community leaders--Illinois--Chicago--Biography. | African Americans--Biography. | Gang members--Illinois--Chicago--Biography. | BISAC BIOGRAPHY & AUTOBIOGRAPHY / Personal Memoirs. | BIOGRAPHY & AUTOBIOGRAPHY / Social Activists | BIOGRAPHY & AUTOBIOGRAPHY / Cultural, Ethnic & Regional / African American & Black
Classification: LCC HN90.C6 .H65 2023 | DDC 323.092--dc23

First Edition
Printed in the United States of America
10 9 8 7 6 5 4 3 2 1

*This book is dedicated to all those
who can relate to this story.*

*A special thanks to Dr. Brent Koch
who helped make this book possible.*

chapter 1

It was a typical midsummer Saturday in July on the South Side of Chicago. I remember the hot sun beating down on my flesh as I made my way out of the house to see where my brothers were. An All-Nation picnic had been planned for my gang and its allies later that afternoon, so I walked down the street repping my gang colors. The Blackstones had become a second family for me, and the black and red t-shirt didn't do me any favors as it absorbed all the sun had to offer. I loved that shirt. The red five-pointed star on the front with the word "Blackstone" across the top gave me a sense of power and pride. The back displayed our slogan, "All is well," along with another five-pointed star, the logo and lettering all in red. I was invincible when I wore that shirt, and isn't that what every fifteen-year-old kid wants?

My mom had taken my brother and sister with her to Hattiesburg, Mississippi, the night before to visit my grandma. I was angry that I wasn't with them. I loved to see my grandma and spend time with all of my family. It was my own fault that I was stuck at home in summer school, but that realization hadn't dawned on me yet. It also meant that I was missing out on the seventeen-hour drive and the 1980s R&B that was playing on whatever FM radio station was being broadcast at the time. I loved Michael Jackson and singing along with the radio.

I took a deep breath and smelled the exhaust fumes mixed with the melting asphalt. Sweat had already begun beading up on my neck as the humidity from Lake Michigan settled in the morning air. It was something you just got used to when you lived on the South Side. Sure, I was a skinny, pimpled-faced kid with a classic late '80s high-top haircut, but I was still good-looking, and I knew it. Today was one of those days that I lived for. Being a part of this gang in this moment was everything to me. Nothing could touch me, and everyone who looked me in the eyes either redirected their gaze or got out of my way.

The All-Nation picnic met at the Dan Ryan Woods, a forest preserve about two miles northwest of my family's home. This 257-acre park off of 87th Street and Western Avenue provided a place for us to come together without interruption. Gang members assembled to tell stories, share handshakes, and talk trash. This was my true family. Sure, my blood family was heading to Mississippi, but these guys were my brothers-in-arms. They knew me and I knew them. Most importantly, when I was with them, I felt no fear. We would do anything for each other.

Members of several different gangs were in attendance—Vice Lords, 4CH, Latin Kings, and others—but today we were the same organization, the same collection. We were all family. The picnic began like any other gathering. A couple games of volleyball, basketball, and softball got started. The various gang t-shirts picked teams, and the competition between us could get heated without anyone really worrying about true violence breaking out. We were just kids for the most part, black and brown kids of various ages just look-ing for a place to belong, a place where we were important and had power and protection. A place that filled the hole each of us had in our hearts. It could have come from abuse, parents who did drugs and were never around, the unbelievable and abject poverty some of us were living in at the time, or it could have just come from kids wanting to be part of something bigger than themselves. For me, the Blackstones had offered a place where I was needed, where I could contribute and wasn't afraid, where people I didn't like feared me, and where those I was closest to loved me like their own. At least that's what I thought.

We ate and shared stories just like we used to do on the porch in the neighborhood where I grew up. One kid would talk about his lat-est girlfriend and what they had been doing the night before. We knew he was probably lying, but the details and daydreams of sexual conquest kept us asking for more. Another kid would talk about the rival gang member he'd beaten up last week or the time he had a gun pulled on him. Car chases, knife fights, and the latest scars and bruises were rites of passage here. The deeper the cut or the better the fight, the more respect you got.

The day was coming to an end, and guys were starting to head back to their various neighborhoods. We parted with handshakes and hugs. Everyone was feeling pretty good from the drinking and from the true sense of belonging that the gang and the picnic had given us.

Darnell, one of the other Blackstones, grabbed me and a couple other guys as we were getting ready to go. He lived about six houses down from me on the same block. Darnell was one of the leaders of the younger guys. Most of the fourteen- to sixteen-year-old kids looked up to him, myself included. He was dark-skinned and short for his age but had a corny charm about him. He was a slick talker and people were drawn to him. We all assumed he wanted to be a pimp by the way he carried himself—slow moving, down to earth, and wearing a cheesy smile that made you want to follow his lead.

He put his arm around me and another guy.

"We're going to go march down the GD streets. You guys in?"

The GDs, or Gangster Disciples, were a rival gang in the same southern Chicago area. While I knew it probably wasn't the best idea to go marching in their neighborhood, I was never afraid when I was with my guys. There were hundreds of us at the All-Nations picnic and the GDs had been messing with the Blackstones and some of the alliance gangs for a couple of weeks. If there was ever a time to do it, it was now. Darnell flashed his toothy smile and we were in. It was time to march.

At least a hundred, maybe more, decided to participate in the street march. I can still see the image of all of us walking down their streets, fearless. We threw up our various gang signs at anyone who looked our way. Anyone who happened to be on the porch or just walking down the street got harassed. No GDs were around yet and we were begging for a fight. Random bystanders got shoved to the pavement, called names, and assaulted if they got in our way.

At one point, a random kid had the poor timing of riding his bike by our march. A Blackstone yelled out, "Hey, kid. Gimme your bike." The kid pedaled faster, trying to get away, and the guy chased him. He wasn't able to catch him until another Blackstone knocked the kid off and kicked him in the head. The kid ran, crying and terrified for his life, as the gang member rode off on the bike, laughing. Another innocent bystander, a forty-year-old woman, walked through the crowd by mistake. One of the guys slapped her, then another, until a whole group of guys were standing around her, slapping and laughing in her face as she covered her head and cried and continued trying to escape the abuse.

I wasn't a part of these interactions, but I didn't stop them either.

I knew that what they were doing to these innocent strangers wasn't right, but I had already told the others I would join the march. I couldn't go back on my word, and I didn't know what would have happened had I tried to intervene. I sure as hell didn't want to find out. By that time, the march had grown so large that most of the guys in and around us were strangers. I didn't need my ass whooped for trying to stop what was already spiraling out of control.

We marched with confidence for a couple more blocks before the GDs figured out what was going on. First there was one gunshot, then another. Random cars came speeding by our march with GDs firing into the crowd. Deion, a Blackstone, raised a 9mm and pulled the trigger to fire a single bullet in the air. I remember thinking, "Why, if the rival gangs are shooting at us, is he shooting into the air?" The coward shouldn't have been there; he should have stayed home. He wasn't a true Blackstone, or he would have been protecting us. Shortly after another spray of bullets, a mad dash ensued as the various gang members fled in all directions.

Jamal, another Blackstone, took off with me. We ran as hard and as fast as we could. Another shot came, then someone screaming, then tires squealing as a sedan did a U-turn in the middle of the street. Still more shots from various pistols. Guys swearing at each other and the sound of fists against flesh. The world spun a little bit as we turned a corner to get away from the chaos and ended up under the 87th Street viaduct.

A skinny, dark-skinned kid no more than 180 pounds came out of nowhere on a bike. I saw Jamal take off across the street and over the railroad tracks. He kept on running and left me by myself with the kid on the bike. I looked around. No one else was around, and I was pissed. The skinny kid jumped off his bike and said, "What the fuck is this on your shirt?" He was talking about the Blackstone logo. He grabbed the shirt again, "What the fuck is this on your shirt?"

I didn't say anything; I just started swinging. Jamal had left me here alone with this skinny kid when we could have easily taken him. We had started a fight by marching up and down their streets together, and I was going to finish it alone. The next thing I knew, I was lying on the ground and wrestling. The kid started to kick me, and it didn't seem like there was anything I could do. Then I saw movement out of the corner of my eye.

Thirty to forty other GDs started running up on us out of nowhere like roaches out of the walls. For the first time since I was seven years old, I was scared—I mean piss-yourself terrified. The type of fear that can only happen when you realize you're about to die and it isn't going to be peaceful. It's going to be the type of death that's going to hurt you and those you care about long after you're gone. We were marching in their streets, we started this, and they weren't going to let me off the hook with a few punches. They were going to murder me on this street in minutes. It was that type of fear.

The GDs picked me up, and I came to the realization that Jamal was there. For some reason, he had turned back, maybe around the time when the first skinny kid was beating on me. I'm not sure because time seemed to slow down and everything got a little blurry. All I knew was that Jamal was there, and I was grateful he hadn't abandoned me.

A trigger clicked, and a deafening shot from a Glock rang in my ears, followed by the hot fumes of sulfur. The world went black as I closed my eyes and recoiled from the sound. I was dead. I had to be. They'd just shot me. That was it. Time stopped. Something splattered across my face and head. I tasted the acidic, salty flavor that could only be the tang of blood. My legs tensed up, and I waited for what-ever was supposed to happen after you were shot to death. I expected searing pain or some sort of sensation that never came.

Then it hit me: the blood I was tasting, it wasn't mine. My eyes opened in time to see Jamal go limp. The back half of his head was gone. He crumbled to the street in an unnatural position as the GDs who were holding his body let him drop. His eyes were open and staring blankly ahead. A primal noise I didn't recognize came out of my mouth, something between a wail and a yell. I pissed my pants. My brain, holding onto some sort of hope and seeing his eyes open, thought, "He's still alive."

Thud! A solid punch in the gut brought me back to reality. Smack! Another hit across the face.

"What the fuck are you doing over here?"

"What's this on your shirt?"

I thought to myself, "Damn! Why did I wear this shirt?"

"Who do you think you are?"

Another voice: "Y'all crazy?"

I hear someone in the background, "Y'all kill that nigga."

More yelling, another punch. I was still alive, but it would be better if I were dead. I screamed again as I saw a hand raise the gun, point the muzzle against my head. Then the trigger was pulled.

Click.

Silence, as forty GDs stare at the gun and then at my head, still fully intact.

I continued screaming, knowing this was the end. The shooter pulled the gun back to inspect the clip and reset the trigger. Another GD put his hand over my mouth to stifle the screams. I got slapped and told to shut up. The shooter raised the gun again, confident he was going to take out another rival gang member.

My eyes widened as the barrel again touched the side of my head, still wet with Jamal's fresh blood. The sweat and filth from the hand over my mouth made me recoil in disgust. I heard the shooter place his finger against the trigger, and I knew this was the end.

Click.

My stomach retched, but I swallowed the bile in my throat. Tears started to roll down my cheeks. Just let it end. I'm tired of being scared. Another GD standing behind the shooter pushed him to the side. He got right up in my face, so close I could smell his breath. He stared into my fear-filled eyes.

"You're a lucky motherfucker."

His eyes broke away from my stare, and I briefly heard the clink of an aluminum bat before I felt the pain of it connecting with the back of my skull. Crack! The pain was blinding and my vision went white. The two GDs holding me let go, and I fell to my knees.

A mid-'80s tan sedan pulled up beside us, and I was pulled back up to my feet. I remember thinking, "Why isn't it over yet?" It was just beginning.

The back driver-side door opened, and I was pulled into the car with my arms held behind my back so I couldn't fight back or move. "What are they doing?" I thought.

I heard the sound of a pocketknife click open. A GD briefly hovered over me with a sadistic smile on his face. I saw the streetlight glint off of the small blade, and then it disappeared into the side of my face. I tried to scream, but my lungs were out of air or had simply given up. The knife carved my cheeks and a line along the back of my head. I felt a tear as my earrings were ripped from my earlobes.

My Blackstone t-shirt, the one I prized so much, was torn and cut as my torturer moved from my face to my chest. He shallowly jabbed the knife into my upper body again and again, all over, piercing the skin but not going deep enough to draw a lot of blood. He alternated between shallow stabs and using the knife to dig up pieces of my skin and muscle. The pain was almost enough to override the terrible dread and fear that I'd been living since I'd first seen the gun. This had to be over soon.

The sadist with the knife seemed to get bored with me and told the others to get me out of the car before any more blood got on the seat. They dragged me out of the car and back to the street where the gang started stomping on me, kicking me in the face and the gut. The guy with the bat was back and started clubbing me in my head and back.

I joined the Blackstones because I had been afraid for most of my life. Fear had guided the majority of the decisions I had made in elementary school and through my adolescence. I was so tired of being afraid and running or turning my back. The Blackstones, the gang life, was a place where I felt safe, where I was protected, and where I would never feel that same level of fear again. The life had protected me—until that day. And in that moment, I recognized a new level of fear I had never felt before.

The bat hit me again. I suffered the pain from the blow and then felt nothing. My body went numb, and my brain told me I had to play dead to get this to end. The fear disappeared as I accepted my fate. I was going to die today. I lay limp and waited.

The beating continued, but I couldn't hear them calling me names, couldn't hear them yelling, or feel their blows. Out of the dull silence I heard a low voice mumble, "That nigga dead," then another followed by a third and more, over and over. A higher voice said, "Let's get the fuck out of here," and the beating ended. They took off in different directions, and I lay there in my own blood, covered in dirt and other people's sweat, savoring the quiet, waiting to die.

What felt like twenty or thirty minutes of beating and fear had all happened in the course of about five minutes. Not long after, a Toyota slowly pulled up alongside my limp body. My only thought was that they had decided to come back to beat me some more or check whether I was actually dead.

A huge black man slowly opened his door and checked over his shoulder. He looked both afraid and worried at the same time and appeared too old to be a gang member, but in my current state, I wasn't sure. He glanced over at Jamal and shook his head. Then he turned to me. He got down on one knee and took my hand.

"Are you okay? Come on, kid. We gotta get you out of here."

I didn't answer. I couldn't believe I was still alive, and my brain told me this guy was just here to finish me off. He was checking to make sure I was dead, and if I wasn't, to finish the job.

He got in my face and grilled me with questions. "What's your name, what's your address, what's your number?"

I groaned. He reached for me, but I didn't want his help. Why would I take help from a guy who was about to kill me?

He kept asking the same questions. He wouldn't get out of my face.

"Kid, we gotta get you out of here. I'm going to help you, but you gotta tell me something so I know where to take you."

I gave in. At this point, what else did I have to lose? I told him I didn't know my name or address, but my mom worked at Christ Hospital. Take me to Christ Hospital.

He reached for me and made an offer to help me get up. He grabbed my arm as I tried to get to my knees. I brushed him aside and yelled, "Man, get off me. I know you're gonna kill me. I don't need your help."

He looked at me with what I can only describe as pity in his eyes. He reached again and told me to calm down. He was going to help me. I told him to help Jamal. He needed it more than me.

His response, "Man, he's dead. I need to help you."

I looked over at Jamal. His eyes were still open. He was covered in blood, but his eyes…He had to be alive. It was then that I realized there was no life in those eyes. I tried to cry, to mourn just a little, but my body had given up so much already. I didn't have it in me.

I was so physically and emotionally exhausted that I couldn't push back on the guy trying to help me anymore. I still didn't trust that he wasn't going to kill me and was just messing with me, but I couldn't stop him from helping me.

"Why haven't you killed me yet?" I asked.

He looked at me and held out his hand.

"I wanna help you," was all he said.

I took his hand as he slowly and gingerly lowered me into the passenger side of his car. I was still scared but had given in as he shut the door. Whatever was going to happen was going to happen. I stayed awake the entire drive to the hospital and watched him, half expecting him to shoot me or pull over and beat me even more. We got to my mom's hospital, and he helped me inside. That was when I realized he wasn't going to kill me, but I was too drained to even thank him. He disappeared as quickly as he had come, and I never saw him again. For all I know, he was my guardian angel.

The hospital staff asked the same questions he had asked. What's my name, what's my address, what's my phone number, but my brain wouldn't fire. I couldn't answer, and they couldn't help me without my basic information. I was put into a sterile bed in the waiting room and left alone, still covered in grime and bleeding. Doctors and nurses rushed around me doing their jobs, but no one paid any attention to me. Occasionally someone would ask my name or my address but would leave when I couldn't answer their questions.

My head pounded as the stark white lights overhead beat down on me. I was tired. My eyelids felt like thousand-pound weights, and all I wanted to do was sleep and give in to the darkness that seemed to be surrounding me. I closed my eyes not knowing what would happen next.

I don't know how much time passed—it may have been minutes or hours—but I do remember feeling someone's gentle touch on my right hand. My eyes gingerly opened, and I saw the stark light again.

Was I dead? No. The pain all over my body told me I was still very much alive. I turned my head and saw a young white girl. She couldn't have been much older than twenty, and her black hair was done up in a ponytail. At first, I thought she was a nurse and was going to ask me a few simple questions and dart off in another direction, but she wasn't dressed like a nurse. She also didn't seem to be in a hurry.

She looked at my ripped Blackstone t-shirt and then back to my face. Her hand held mine gently but firmly, and she seemed content to wait for me to come out of my haze. I let my eyes fall shut again.

"No, honey. You can't go to sleep," I heard her say. I knew she was right next to me, but her voice sounded far away. I opened my eyes again. She smiled.

"I know this is hard for you, but you need to try to remember your name, your address, anything to help the doctors figure out who you are. You're going to lie here and die if you can't, and I won't let that happen."

She paused and smiled again.

"So what's your name?"

I couldn't come up with my own damn name. I was defeated. I was done, and all I wanted to do was fall asleep. I didn't know this lady, and I didn't want her help. She didn't leave; she just sat there holding my hand and occasionally asking me my name or address. She wouldn't let me fall asleep. I wanted to remember my name. I wanted help, but I couldn't think of any way to help her or myself. I just wanted to sleep. With tears streaming out of the corners of my eyes, I gave up. I let my eyelids fall, and I felt the warmth and the peace of the sleep wrap me in its embrace.

Then I heard the "click" of the gun misfire, and my eyes shot open.

"My name is William."

chapter 2

My mom met my dad during her senior year at Englewood High School in Chicago. He was a basketball player working through his junior year. She was hanging out with her friends after school on a random afternoon, and he happened to be hanging out with a couple of teammates. He approached her with one of his friends beside him. In typical wingman fashion, his friend started a conversation with my mom's friend, so my dad could start talking with my mom. That's how their relationship began. No fanfare, no love at first sight, just a simple conversation after school.

Growing up, Mom had ten siblings. They were all lighter skinned, but she was very dark and struggled through her entire childhood because of this. White and black kids made fun of her equally. She wasn't accepted by either group, and that had a lasting impact on her social status and mental health. Kids used to call her names like "charcoal" and "blackie" along with others. She obviously didn't feel white, but she also didn't feel black because no one accepted her, and that was all she really wanted. Her deepest pain was the fact that her own peers didn't accept her because of her color.

That was her life throughout elementary, middle, and most of high school. I say most because in 1968, her senior year, the iconic "Godfather of Soul," James Brown, released the song "Say It Loud—I'm Black and I'm Proud," and things started to change for her. With the release of that song, it became acceptable and almost enviable to have darker skin. She was voted "Dark-Skinned Miss Englewood" that year, and finally had her first real taste of acceptance.

My dad and mom started dating, but Mom was already seeing a serviceman. As my parent's relationship got more serious, my dad asked my mom to break it off with the other guy. He was on a military base, and they didn't have regular contact, so she sent a simple Dear John letter to call off the relationship. Shortly after, my mom became pregnant with my older brother, Phil. According to her, she didn't want to get married, but my dad asked her to. She sought advice from her father, and he told her that it was her decision to make. My dad told me that her father forced him to propose because he'd gotten her pregnant. In March of 1969, they got married.

They lived together and worked odd jobs for a couple of years before moving to Washington Heights in May of 1971. They were the fifth black family in the neighborhood. Mom told me they picked the area and block because it was safe, it was clean, and it was a good family environment. My sister, Sharon, was born a couple of years after my brother, and a couple of years after that, I came along.

The house I grew up in was a brick bungalow in the center of Washington Heights. Three of the four bedrooms were on the main level, along with the kitchen, living room, one full bathroom, and dining room, and there was another bedroom and full bathroom in the basement. It also had an attic we used for storage. I stayed out of it because it creeped me out. The open, hot, and dark space scared me. The front door opened to the living room, and we had radiators that were used to heat the home in the winter. There wasn't central air, so we had window units that cooled the house when it got too hot to leave the windows open.

Hardwood floors were spread throughout the various rooms. The living room connected to the dining room, which connected through another door to the small kitchen. Our refrigerator was in the corner, the stove right next to it, and a small counter and sink beside it. White wooden cupboards supported the countertop, and a beige, square, vinyl backsplash ran about two-thirds up the wall around most of the kitchen. In the main-level bathroom, baby pink was everywhere. The toilet cover was pink, the walls had light pink tiles, and the hand towels were pink. It was well-coordinated, but man, was it pink.

My bedroom was pretty normal. I shared it with my brother, and we each had a twin bed. We had so many Michael Jackson posters on the wall, we could barely see the wood paneling beneath them. There was a wooden staircase with a makeshift rail that led to the basement from the kitchen. The washer and dryer were located at the bottom of the stairs along with an open space for the fourth bedroom. The basement bathroom was even more pink than the main-level one. Brighter pink tiles ran from the ceiling to the cement floor. A small sink sat on top of a converted classic seventies-style cabinet. The cabinet had sliding doors with a small hole in each upper corner that you could slip your finger into to pull the doors along the rail that held them. A mirror with vertical lights hung above the sink. The basement had the normal utility storage closet and was considered finished, but it didn't have much more than a concrete floor, some wood paneling on the walls, and some leftover cabinets that had been hung for additional storage.

The backyard was a good size for being in the city, and it led to a single detached garage. A chain-link fence ran down both sides of the narrow lot in the backyard to define the property line and provide some peace of mind for my mom when we were outside. There was also a concrete slab directly outside the back door that provided a gathering space on hot summer nights. The front of the house featured a concrete staircase that led to the front door. This staircase, what my family and I referred to as the porch, became a nightly gathering place throughout my childhood.

Houses in our neighborhood were built practically one on top of the other. They were so close, we could hear the neighbor kids getting whooped even with our windows closed. This meant the neighbors could also hear when we were getting our beatings. We would share these experiences with each other the next day. Sometimes, we'd offer comfort, but most of the time, we'd make fun of one another or our parents.

Some of my earliest, and fondest, memories are of sitting on the front porch of our house. Every night around six, various families would gather on their porches to share stories and watch the kids play in the street. Kids would dance and play games between the infrequent cars that passed by. My mom found acceptance in our neighborhood through the front porch. She started to get involved in everything she could. If the neighbors wanted to have a block party, she chaired the committee to organize it and made sure it was the best one they had ever experienced. PTO needed volunteers? Count her in. She finally had a group of friends who accepted her, and that became one of the most important things in her life.

Mom and Dad got divorced when I was four years old. I was too young at the time to really understand what was going on or why it was happening. My brother, sister, mom, and I all stayed at the Washington Heights house, and my dad moved to Hazel Crest, IL. The front porch was still a safe and fun place for us to get together. The structure provided a kind of safety and comfort I didn't fully comprehend at the time. It sheltered not only my experiences, but my reality as well. I couldn't see how the neighborhood was changing or what was happening beyond my world on that porch.

My siblings and I adjusted to our new family existence. We had less supervision with Mom working all the time, but she still ran a tight ship and expected things done her way and on time. We each had our own specific chores and a very detailed way they were to be completed in order to be considered done to her standards. If we didn't do something just right, we were punished. There were even times when we busted our asses to do everything perfectly, and she would come home from work and still be in a bad mood. The house would be sparkling, I mean almost literally sparkling, but she would look under the radiator, find one little dust bunny, and go off. If we were lucky, it would just be screaming and yelling. Not so lucky, and the belt would come out and we'd get whooped.

Her expectations also extended to our grades. She wanted the perfect house with the straight-A kids to show the world how great she was at being a mother. It didn't matter what was happening in our personal lives or behind the scenes, as long as it looked right on the outside. There was no praise or reward for meeting her standards or expectations, only punishments for falling short.

The punishment wasn't always something physical. Sometimes it was withholding new clothes or a new pair of name-brand shoes, especially from me. I'd beg and tell her I needed the right clothes or I would get made fun of and bullied at school, but it didn't matter. If I screwed up, I was going to be punished for it in whatever way she deemed appropriate. Other times, we got grounded and sent to our rooms. It all depended on Mom's mood and what exactly we had or hadn't done. It only got worse after the divorce as my mom was working more and more to pay the bills and provide for our family.

Buddy showed up shortly after my parents got divorced. It turns out my mom had dated him prior to my father, but they had broken up for reasons she'd never shared with me. She hadn't thought about him or seen him in years. One afternoon, when she was leaving Christ Hospital after a long shift, she happened to run into him on the sidewalk. At first glance, she didn't recognize him, but he knew her smile immediately. They started talking and rekindled a spark that hadn't quite died when they'd broken up all those years ago.

Buddy was a musician and specialized in the trombone. He was a lighter-skinned guy and had a big mustache. He kept the rest of his face clean-shaven but was proud of that bushy upper lip. Always a quiet guy and kind of a nerd, he was living with his ailing father when my mom got back together with him. His weight seemed to fluctuate depending on his stress and emotional state, but he was never a big guy.

As kids, we welcomed this new male figure into our home. Mom was working too much and still struggling to pay the bills. There were many nights during the cold of winter when we would sleep in the same room together in order to stay warm. Having the extra income meant our lives could get back to a somewhat normal routine while also having an adult at home while Mom was off at work.

My brother, sister, and I loved having Buddy around. He was really affectionate and willing to play games with us. Even before he officially moved in with us, he would come to the house after school or on the weekends. I think it provided him an occasional escape from being with his father, whose cancer was taking over his body. We'd get home from school and have a wrestling match or play fight with him. He made us laugh, and he loved to tickle us. To pass the time, he would draw and tell us stories. Sure, Mom wasn't around—she was either working at one of her multiple jobs or planning the next community get-together—but Buddy was there to fill in the gaps. We trusted and liked him, and he liked being around us.

The cancer eventually won and took Buddy's dad. He was

devastated after the loss, and depression quickly followed. He asked to move in with us, and my mom agreed. She felt sorry for him, and she didn't want him to be in his home alone after his father had died. I think she also thought that being around us would help him with the depression that seemed to be worsening by the day. At first, that seemed to be the case. He would still want to wrestle or tickle fight or draw with us, but he never did deal with the depression or the demons that came with it.

Our basement seemed to be his refuge. He would disappear down there for hours at a time when my mom wasn't around, smoking weed, watching TV, or working to build his own computer. He'd still come up for meals or to check on us, but he wasn't as happy as he'd been when he and my mom had first gotten back together. It didn't matter much to me or my siblings what he was doing with his time as long as he treated us well and was around, but it was becoming more and more rare to actually see my mom at home.

After Buddy moved in, money wasn't as big of an issue anymore. He had a good job and was able to help with the bills. Sure, there were some lean times now and then, but we never knew it. That didn't stop my mom from working two jobs, from always wanting a little more, and from being away from the house more than she was in it. When she wasn't working, she was with her new group of friends planning and organizing the next event for the neighborhood or the church or the school. Occasionally she'd announce she was going on a trip or a cruise with her friends. I found out later in life that a lot of the extra work she took on, the need for that second job, was so she could fund these trips with her friends. These people accepted her, and that meant more to her than hanging out with her family.

Shortly after he'd moved in with us, Buddy had asked my mom to marry him, but she didn't want to. My brother and sister kept bugging her and asking her when she was going to say yes. Then the church members started asking. After all, she was living in sin having a man in her house without being married to him. The pressure of the church combined with the mounting questions from us kids pushed her to eventually give in, and they got married. I had a step-dad who wanted me around and liked spending time with me. What more could a young kid want?

Despite his vices and his ongoing battle with depression, Buddy treated me and my siblings well and took care of our mom. When we would visit my dad, we would tell him all about the things we had been doing with Buddy. We would share all of the good experiences and let him know how much we loved Buddy, even going as far as to say he was a good man and that we were glad he was in our home. Dad would smile and say he was happy for us, but I knew it hurt him.

As I got older and the porch provided less protection, I began to understand what was really happening in the streets of our idyllic neighborhood. My view of the world was less obstructed, and my eyes could actually take in what was going on around me. Our neighbors started to leave, and new people moved in. I didn't know enough at the time to understand who was leaving or to ask why. My family noticed a lot of white people selling their homes and leaving the neighborhood to be replaced by minority homeowners. My brother and sister noticed, at least. Mom wasn't home enough to see it happening. Construction began on a low-income housing project a couple of years later. My neighborhood went from a safe place with parties and neighbors hanging out on their front porches to a place of fear and control. A place where people with power took what they wanted without repercussions, and the rest of us simply gave in.

I vividly remember getting a brand-new bike when I turned six. My mom surprised both me and my brother with a couple of Schwinns. It was one of the first brand-new things I had ever received.

My brother's was red, and mine was blue. I loved that bike and the freedom it gave me to explore my neighborhood and the various alleys and side streets that surrounded my home. We usually rode in the alleys because there was no traffic, which meant we could ride without worrying about getting hit by a car. The bikes were the closest things to independence that our ten- and six-year-old minds could comprehend, and we loved to ride around the neighborhood to show off our new wheels.

My brother was faster than I given he had four years on me. We would race down the alleys, and I always tried to beat him but could never quite pull it off. One afternoon, we were racing up and down the alley closest to our house when he came to an abrupt stop. I nearly ran into the back of his bike as I skidded my tires, just missing his back wheel with my front. Directly in front of us, at the end of the alley, was a group of kids on bikes. I didn't recognize any of them. They were older than me, and I couldn't tell if they were from our neighborhood or not.

One of the kids was about the same size as me. He waved off the rest of the pack, and they sped down the alley and headed left onto the street. He approached me and my brother and asked if he could ride my bike. I was young and naïve and didn't think twice about his request. I was proud of that bike, and if someone else wanted to ride it and tell me how great it was, who was I to stop them? My brother gave me a sideways glance that I couldn't interpret. He looked a little concerned but was trying to hide it with a smile.

I got off the bike and handed it to the kid. He got on and headed down and around the side of the alley. I felt slightly nervous as he rode farther and farther down the pavement and closer to the end of the block, but then I realized my brother still had his bike and there were two of us to only one of him. Just as I thought my brother was going to take off in pursuit, the kid stopped, turned, and started riding back. He pulled up alongside me and hopped off my bike.

"Nice bike," he said.

"Thanks. Can I have it back?" I asked, trying to hide my excitement that he liked the bike.

He handed it over, and I got back on, both pleased that he had liked the bike and ready to ride away the rest of the afternoon. Then I noticed that he was still holding onto one handlebar. I pulled a little and wiggled it, thinking he had forgotten he was holding on, but his grip tightened, and I looked up at him. He smiled, and I awkwardly smiled back. Then he kicked me straight in the stomach, and I fell backward to the cement.

The wind had been knocked out of me, and I gasped for breath as my butt hit the pavement. My vision got clouded as the tears started to well in my eyes from the pain in my gut. I fell to my side and let the tears fall as I realized what was happening. He was stealing my bike. Out of the corner of my eye, I saw a flash of movement. My brother's tires raced by my head as he took off after the kid. He was moving, letting loose, and doing everything he could to catch up. It looked like he was about to catch him when they both turned left at the end of the alley and out of my sight. I continued to lay on the ground, drawing shallow breaths as tears ran down my cheeks, hoping my brother would get my bike back.

I heard some yelling from the end of the block—my brother and another voice. He must have caught that kid and was getting my bike back! I rolled over to see what was going on, but they were still around the corner. The shouting stopped, and I sat up to peer down the alley. What was going on? My brother appeared and started walking toward me with his hands in his pockets. He wasn't riding his bike, and he sure as hell didn't have mine. Every now and then, he'd glance back over his shoulder and pick up his pace as he walked back to me. I sat up, trying to figure out what was happening. He came up to me with a look of both fear and anger on his face. He frowned a little bit when he saw the tears on my cheeks and reached out his hand to help me up.

"What happened?" I asked.

"I had his ass, Will. I caught him and I was going to pound him to get your bike back. But when I turned the corner, the other kids that were with him were still there. They didn't leave. They had just ridden down the street a way. The entire gang of them was still there."

It was then that I understood the look on his face and why he had been nervous. He wanted to make sure they weren't following him.

"The little kid that took your bike pulled up alongside them," my brother said. "One of the other bigger kids without a bike walked toward me and told me to get off. I told him no way and to give me your bike back. The kids all laughed at me, then the big kid took hold of the handlebars and told me to get off my bike again. I told him hell no and tried to pull away."

My brother's voice trailed off and he looked back over his shoulder again.

I pulled his hand and asked him what happened next.

His focus came back to me, but so did the fear on his face. "The kid pulled a knife on me, and told me to give him the bike or he'd kill me."

I knew my face couldn't hide the fear and concern I was feeling. My eyes got really big, and I looked my brother up and down to make sure he hadn't been cut.

"Are you okay?" I asked.

"Yeah, I'm fine. But they took my bike too."

Relieved that my brother was okay but overcome with anger, I dropped his hand from mine and threw both my arms in the air. "Wait, we *both* got our bikes stolen?" I shouted in my high-pitched, pre-adolescent voice.

"Yep. We both got our bikes stolen."

"Man, ain't that a bitch?"

My brother started laughing. He put his arm around me and we continued our walk home, coming up with all sorts of plans for what we would do to those kids if we ever saw them again.

We got home and told our mom how the entire situation went down. My brother thought he recognized one of the kids from the neighborhood high school. We got out an old yearbook and looked through each class, page-by-page and picture-by-picture until we found him. Mom took us to the police station to file our stolen bike reports. A couple of days later, the cops found the kids still riding our bikes and we got them back. I had never been so happy as I was to see those blue and red Schwinns.

This was my first real encounter with what our neighborhood was changing into. Kids, some as young as six years old, were already stealing what they wanted. Fights became more frequent as did the influence of drugs and gun violence. The porch provided little protection, and I started to look inside my home for additional guidance on how to stay safe. It was clear that the streets and neighborhood around me were not going to be a positive influence moving forward. This was the backdrop for some of my earliest memories, and the impact of this environment would have a huge influence on my personality and decisions over the next several years. Looking back, I wish I could have seen what was coming.

chapter 3

Despite the occasional bike theft and the strict routine my mom kept, I was a happy kid. I loved music, especially Michael Jackson. He was my musical idol. I mean, it was the '80s, and he was the King of Pop!

Our neighborhood block would hold talent shows during the summer. My mom would help organize these types of events, and to keep things fair, they would break down the categories by age. The same summer my bike was stolen, I entered the kids division of the show and did an entire Jackson routine. I sang and danced my ass off and ended up winning my category. It's one of the few times I can remember my mom telling me she was proud of me.

Buddy had been living with us for a while after he and my mom had gotten married. My siblings and I were excited to have him in our lives and to have a more permanent father figure around. He took us places and built a real, trusting relationship with each of us. I loved to wrestle with him, and his jokes always made me laugh. He encouraged my musical talents given his own musical hobbies. He would have me sing and perform concerts for him in the basement, and I loved having an audience.

He spent a lot of time down there, working on the personal computer he was trying to build or watching TV. I didn't realize it at the time, but the smell constantly hanging in the air was from his weed habit. The basement was his refuge and his place in our house. He was always down there, working on that computer, smoking weed, or just letting the day go by. Because of this, it didn't take me by surprise when he called me downstairs one afternoon.

My favorite song at the time was Michael Jackson's "Off the Wall." I had every lyric memorized and could hit every note on pitch. (Did I mention that I loved Michael Jackson?) I was wearing a pair of Spider-Man pajamas that day, the kind of pajamas that looked like a costume, complete with a mask. I can still hear Buddy's voice calling out as he heard me dancing on the floor above his head.

"Hey, Will."

I heard him but didn't acknowledge. I was too busy dancing.

His voice came a little louder: "Will!"

I stopped dancing and yelled back down. "Huh?"

"Come downstairs for a minute."

I pulled off my mask, wondering what he wanted. "Okay," I hollered back.

I half-ran to the stairs and placed my hands against opposite walls, holding most of my weight so I could skip down the stairs, as most seven-year-olds would, my tongue hanging out of my mouth and a big, goofy smile on my face. I leaped over the last few steps and landed on the cool basement floor. Buddy wasn't in his normal chair or hunched over the computer like I expected, but I could still smell the pungent weed hanging in the air.

"Hey, Will," he called from the bathroom. "Come in here."

I remember thinking for a brief moment, *That's weird...come in there*. I wonder why he wants me to go in there, but I brushed it off. After all, I was only seven and I trusted him.

I opened the bathroom door and saw him standing there, facing me. He stared at me with an expression I had never seen before and haven't seen since. It was as if he was looking at me but also through me—his face completely blank, empty. I glanced over my shoulder to see what he was staring at, but only saw the wall. I looked back at him. He hadn't moved and his expression hadn't changed. I smiled awkwardly, trying to figure out what was happening and why I was in the bathroom with him.

He stood there a moment longer. His gaze and his eyes occasionally shifting from looking directly at me to whatever he was looking at behind me. He was deep in thought. I realized later that he was trying to figure out what he was going to do next and how he was going to do it. Then he stared directly at me for a long time, and a smile slowly formed across his face.

When he finally spoke, his voice had changed. He normally spoke to me like any other person he was talking to. That was something I really liked about him. He treated me like a grown-up and didn't talk down to me or speak to me like I was a little kid. Not usually. But this time it was different. He wanted something and decided the best way to get it was to treat me like the seven-year-old I was.

In a higher, almost excited tone, he asked, "Hey, Will. I want you to do something for me, okay?"

I raised an eyebrow. His tone had caught me off-guard. Usually, I would be all-in, expecting a tickle fight or a chance to wrestle, but something felt different this time.

"Like what?" I managed.

"Let me show you something right quick," he said, reaching for my pajamas.

He grabbed my pajama pants and pulled them down to my ankles.

Then he started rubbing on my privates.

I didn't know what was going on or why he was doing this. My brain couldn't comprehend the situation. It felt wrong and gross, but I trusted him and he had never done anything like this before. What was happening?

Buddy looked up at me with that weird smile on his face. "How does that feel?" he asked.

I didn't answer. I didn't know what to say to him. I was so confused, and my stomach was starting to hurt.

Buddy stood up and pulled down his own pants and underwear. He stood there naked from the waist down and looked at me. Then he asked me to rub him the way he had been rubbing me. His voice was still playful, but his tone had changed. While he had asked me to do it, I knew it wasn't a request. He was telling me.

My fingers reached out slowly, and I touched him. My stomach heaved, and I pulled my hand back. He looked at me, and the smile was gone. I reached my hand back out again and touched him. I wasn't sure what he wanted me to do or why. He was starting to grow impatient and looked annoyed. Then the smile came back, and he brushed my hand away. He put his hand on my shoulder and suggested that I put my mouth on his privates. Seven-year-olds can't hide feelings or emotions. My face immediately distorted into a confused and shocked expression. Why would I want to do that?

"Go ahead, Will," he said. "It's okay." His tone had changed back to playful, almost childlike.

I felt my body starting to shake, a mixture of complete terror at what was happening and a sickness building in my stomach.

He coached me forward. "Go ahead, Will. It'll be okay."

I wanted to throw up. I wanted to run away. I wanted to be anywhere else other than that basement. I wanted to be back at the top of the stairs, dancing to Michael Jackson and singing in my

Spider-Man pajamas, anywhere but this awful pink basement bathroom.

I don't remember much about what happened next. I think my mind has permanently blocked that out to help protect me. The next thing I remember, he had finished and told me it was okay to go upstairs as I was pulling up my pajama bottoms. That's all I needed to hear—the permission to leave. I bounded up the stairs as fast as I could.

Then I heard him call after me and chase me up the stairs. I froze, completely terrified. Had I done it wrong? What was he going to do? Was he going to make me do more, or was he going to hurt me? The fear was so overwhelming, I couldn't move. I just stood there and waited for him to catch me. He grabbed my shoulder like he had done in the basement. He handed me a dollar. That weird smile was back.

"I'll give you this dollar if you don't tell no one about what just happened."

My mind, still frozen in fear, told my arm to reach out and take it. My face was devoid of emotions as I reached out. Buddy, sensing that I wasn't all there or entirely hearing what he said, pulled the dollar back. He ripped it in half and put one half in my hand.

"You'll get the other half when I know you're not going to tell anyone," he said. His tone was no longer playful. He was back to speaking to me like I was an adult. He turned and walked back downstairs.

I stood there for a minute, looking at the crumpled half of a dollar in my hand. I caught some movement out of the left side of my eye and turned my head. My sister was standing there, just down the hall. I didn't know how long she had been there or what she had heard or seen. She didn't move or say anything. I turned right and went to my bedroom.

I lay in my bed the rest of the afternoon. I couldn't move. I didn't cry. I simply lay there thinking about what had happened and trying to figure out why. The entire experience kept playing over and over again in my head. Feeling the basement walls on my fingertips as I bounded down the stairs to see what Buddy wanted. The uneasy feeling I'd gotten when he had called me into the bathroom. The way he'd stared at me and touched me. What he had made me do to him. The stupid ripped dollar bill still in my hand. I couldn't shake the fear that had been planted in my mind. I was no longer comfortable in my own home, and I didn't know what I was going to do. I'd gone down those stairs that afternoon a happy and carefree seven-year-old; I'd come up them a very different person. I was scared and alone. I didn't know what to do or who to trust. My world no longer made sense and I had nowhere to turn.

It didn't stop there. Over the next several months, Buddy would force me and my sister to watch *Behind the Green Door*, a pornographic film from the early '70s. I believe he wanted us to pay attention to certain scenes so we could be better at pleasuring him. We hated that movie and watching it with him, but we didn't have a choice with him being the only adult in the home. Glued to the TV, my brain got used to watching porn like it was a sitcom. It normalized sex and made me want to see more and more naked women at a very young age.

Whether or not I realized it at the time—I don't remember when I did—my worldview and how I reacted to things had profoundly changed and would continue to change. Every new experience that came along shaped me and gave me a choice. Every choice led to a different experience and set of rewards or consequences. Going downstairs when Buddy had called for me was one choice. Coming up and not telling anyone about what had happened with him was another. These experiences and actions had a direct impact on who I was becoming and what I was about to become over the next several years.

chapter 4

It's strange being a seven-year-old and not feeling safe in your own home. In my mind, the people I was supposed to trust and turn to when I needed support or help had abandoned me. My older brother, Phil, was starting to figure out what path he wanted to take and who he wanted to be. He no longer had any time for childish games or the things I was interested in. Mom continued to work and go on trips with her friends. My sister was around, but she couldn't offer the support or guidance that a father figure could. I was alone and scared with nowhere to turn.

My cousin, Quinton, and his mom moved into our house around the same time the molestation began. Quinton's mom needed some financial support and couldn't get a place on her own. We had some extra space in the basement, and the money they paid for rent helped our family in the short-term. Quinton provided light in my life during a time of deep darkness.

I was a year older than Quinton, and I enjoyed having someone around who looked up to me. The two of us, along with my other cousin, GJ, were tight. *The Three Amigos* movie came out that same year, so naturally, we called ourselves by the same title. We were inseparable that summer. Whether Quinton knew it at the time, him coming to live with us might have saved my life.

We ran around the block and streets of our neighborhood together like any seven- and eight-year-old would do with minimal parental supervision. We didn't get into any real trouble, just normal, dumb, adolescent things that helped us pass the time while our moms were at work. We loved to make up songs, and we called ourselves "The Doo-Wop Boys" as most of our songs had some good front porch, doo-wop lines that were popular in '50s and '60s pop music.

Our songs weren't anything groundbreaking, but we'd take turns making up lyrics as we walked around the neighborhood. Anything that caught our attention or happened around us could be turned into a "doo-wop" song.

"Doo-doo-wop, woah-ohh-ohhh, doo-doo-wop. There's a can rolling down the street. Doo-wop. I'm gonna kick it with my feet. Woah, doo-wop."

We'd laugh, and then the other one would continue with the next line of lyrics: "Doo-wop, mmm-mm, doo-wop-wop. Look at those dogs humping with one on top. Doo-wop. I wonder if they'll ever stop? Mmm, doo-wop."

The dogs humping made us both laugh so hard, we couldn't keep singing and had to stop to catch our breath.

I still loved music, and I enjoyed performing. Quinton always told me I was the entertainer in the family. I could dance and I could sing. Whenever there were family picnics, reunions, or get-togethers, I would always be asked to put on a show or provide some entertainment. Performing always won my mom's pride, and it also got me the positive attention I was so desperately seeking at home.

Quinton could sing, too, but he wasn't as good as I was. Most of our shows would be the two of us singing or dancing. My favorite was singing Michael Jackson's "Say Say Say." It was a duet with Jackson and Paul McCartney. Quinton was Paul, and I would be Michael. Our families would clap and sing along with us, and they would always give us a lot of applause when we finished our set. When Quinton was around, I felt normal, like there was someone else I could talk to who supported me.

About a year after they moved in, Quinton's mom had saved enough to get their own apartment in the Southshore neighborhood. I went from seeing Quinton literally every day to only on Sundays for church or other family functions organized by my grandma. A short while after that, they ended up moving back to Mississippi, following my mom's parents. They could see the neighborhood changing, the gangs and drugs starting to fill the streets. They were smart and got out early. I wished I could go with them, but my family remained in Chicago, and Buddy remained in our basement.

My brother, sister, and I did the best we could with our situation. I avoided Buddy by playing in the streets with my friends and would do whatever I could to do my chores when he wasn't around. Mom still had her expectations of how clean the house should be and what needed to be done in order to avoid a whooping or other punishment.

We got pretty good at cooking for ourselves, and one of our favorite snacks was homemade French fries. We had to make them on our own while Buddy was sleeping since he was working nights and my mom was at work during the day. Phil and I would cut the potatoes into fries, and my sister was in charge of dropping them into the hot oil.

Sharon would tell us, "You cut 'em, I'll cook 'em," and Phil and I would get to work. We were eating them about as fast as we could make them, and we kept wanting more and more. They were some damn good fries! We kept eating and eventually Sharon fried up the final batch. She put them on a plate with some paper towels to sop up any leftover grease and sprinkled them with some salt. We sat down to eat and smiled—we were finally full. All of us leaned back in our chairs, and I thanked both of them for making the fries.

Then Sharon wrinkled her nose and sniffed the air. "What's that smell?" she asked.

I inhaled and smelled the distinct odor of burning, but I didn't know what from.

Phil jumped up, a wild panic in his eyes. "Shit!" he yelled. "The pan is on fire!"

I looked over at the stovetop to confirm he was right. The pan with the fry grease in it was burning, boiling over and catching fire on the burner below. Sharon had forgotten to turn off the stove.

Phil ran to the stove and turned off the burner, but it was too late. The fire had reached the top of the pan, and the entire top was burning wildly. We all watched the flames grow higher and higher. Phil panicked and ran to the sink and turned on the water to let it fill up. Then he grabbed the hot pan and threw it in. Even at my young age, I knew you shouldn't throw water on a grease fire, but apparently in his state of panic, Phil had forgotten. A smoky fireball shot up from the pan, looking like a nuclear bomb going off in our kitchen.

I'd like to say that I was the hero who kept a cool head and had got the fire under control, but I cannot. When I saw those flames hit the ceiling, I took off, screaming at the top of my lungs. "We gotta get out of here! We're all gonna die! Call the police!" I screamed as I ran out the kitchen door and into the yard.

I got outside and ran down the sidewalk a little way, still screaming before I realized no one was following me. I remember thinking, "You think I'm gonna stay in this bitch, you lost your mind," but I wanted to make sure my brother and sister were okay, so I turned around and started back to the house. By the time I got back to the kitchen door, they had successfully put the fire out. Sharon had kept her cool and remembered that the fire wouldn't continue burning without oxygen, so they'd thrown towels on that pan like you see people throw money at strippers. The fire was out, but the damage to the kitchen had been done.

We looked around at the soot on the walls and the ceiling. It was everywhere.

"Mom is gonna kill us," said Sharon.

"Uh-huh," was all I could say.

Buddy came out of the bedroom and took in the damage. His mouth kind of hung open as he tried to figure out what was going on. "What the hell happened?" he finally managed to ask.

I wanted to say we were trying to kill your perverted ass, but thought better of it. Phil eventually explained about the fry grease and how he and Sharon had gotten the fire under control.

When Phil finished the story, Buddy half-laughed and said, "Well, you better get this cleaned up before your mom gets home or she's gonna whoop your asses." Then he turned and headed back to the bedroom.

"Some help he was," Phil said, shaking his head as he looked around the kitchen.

"What are we gonna do?" I asked. This was a big mess, and I knew none of us knew how to clean soot off of the walls.

"We're gonna paint it," Sharon said so confidently that neither of us questioned the idea.

In the garage, we found some old, white paint that the previous owners of the house had used for the exterior before they'd sold it to us. Phil grabbed a small brush and did the detail work while Sharon and I used rollers and a wide brush to paint the larger spaces. We painted the entire kitchen and down the hallway because the wall continued down the hall without a break for us to stop. Phil even did the ceiling to hide the aftermath of the fireball he'd set off.

All three of us were pretty proud of our work, but we knew we would need an explanation for Mom when she got home. Phil decided the best idea would be to tell her we had decided to do it as a surprise because she had been working so hard. It made sense to Sharon and me, so we finished our regular chores and deep-cleaned the house more than we ever had in the past.

Mom got home at her normal time, and the three of us were waiting at the front door to greet her. We pulled her into the kitchen and yelled "Surprise!" to help sell the idea that we had done this out of good and honest intentions.

Boy was she surprised, but she wasn't stupid. She told Sharon we'd done a good job painting, but then started asking us all kinds of questions about why we had decided to paint the kitchen and the hallway. I'm still not sure how she figured out what had really happened. To this day, neither Phil nor Sharon have confessed that they'd told Mom any story other than the one the three of us had agreed upon.

The extension cord came out, and we got the type of whooping that would alarm family services today. We all hated that cord and the way my Mom was able to hit us with it. To make it worse, we each had to watch as she beat our other siblings. I was usually last because I was the youngest, and the anticipation, along with seeing Phil and Sharon get whooped, was almost worse than the beating itself.

Worse still, after we had been sent to bed, we heard her talking to a girlfriend on the phone. She paused after telling her friend the story. It seemed like she was trying to decide whether she was impressed with our actions or still upset. I should have known better than to hope for anything other than disappointment, and we finally heard her exclaim, "I ain't givin' them no love for this." If I were a betting man, I'd put money on Buddy telling her the whole story. It still kind of pisses me off that we'd gotten a beating after she'd told

Sharon how well we had painted everything.

That was the ongoing problem with me and my mom. Sure, we'd done something wrong, but it had been an honest accident, and we'd tried to fix it, but that still wasn't enough. In my eyes, we could never get any love for anything. I didn't think we were going to get in trouble because we'd fixed the mistake. We'd painted the kitchen and made it look better than when we'd moved in. We had corrected our error. We were growing up.

My mother has expressed concern with how she might be portrayed in this book, and I told her I was simply going to share what I felt and experienced. The thing I wanted more than anything growing up in that home was love and support. She had her own demons from her childhood that she never ended up dealing with. Those demons continued to haunt her, and eventually, they started to haunt her children. In the end, it seemed like every time there could have been a smile, an opportunity for praise, or at the very least, a simple hug, the situation instead turned to tears. Every time she could have given us love, she decided not to, and I was tired of crying.

chapter 5

The next several years blurred together in the same pattern. I tried to avoid being home as much as I could so I wouldn't have to see Buddy. My brother and I grew even further apart as he was trying to figure who he was and wanted to be. He didn't have time for his younger brother, and though I desperately wanted a male figure to look up to, he just wasn't around. For all I knew, he was avoiding the house for the same reason I was. Sharon and I didn't talk much after the basement incident. Every now and then, Buddy would call her downstairs, and I could only imagine what he was doing to her. I wanted to help her, but I didn't know how or what to do.

I started getting into trouble at school. Kids would make fun of me for my clothes or would call my mom names. The only way I knew to counter the situation was to fight. I was already incredibly insecure because of what I had been exposed to, and hearing kids call my mom "Blackie" or getting made fun of for wearing the same clothes twice in one week or having holes in my shoes sent me over the edge.

Mom didn't like that I was getting in fights. She always told me to walk away or just ignore the other kids. I can still hear her say, "William, it's just words. You don't have to fight." But she wasn't there, and she didn't get it. Why couldn't she sympathize with me after she had been made fun of most of her childhood for the color of her skin? It wasn't like she didn't know what was going on because I told her whenever I could. It wasn't enough and, in the end, I didn't want to come home knowing that Buddy was sitting in the basement, maybe in the bathroom, while Mom worked late or was off with her friends.

I felt completely alone and vulnerable. I didn't have any support from my family, and the only way I gained any respect at school was to fight. But the more I fought, the more upset my mom would get. She wasn't actually concerned with the fact that I was fighting. Her concern was the constant worry about what other people would think of her. She had the kid who was always getting in trouble at school, and that was the last thing she wanted her friends thinking. I'd beg her to talk to the teachers or the principal, to do anything to help me stop the bullying, but she'd just continue preaching the walk-away approach.

When I realized she wasn't going to support me, I asked if she could get me some new clothes to at least help with the name-calling about the hand-me-downs I was currently wearing. She told me to get my grades up and stop fighting, and she would see what she could do. I knew that the constant harassment wouldn't stop without some-thing giving on her end, so I asked for a minimum of one new pair of sneakers. It was the '80s, after all, and shoe fashion was even more important than the rest of my clothes back then. She consented and said she would take me to Payless. I begged her for anything but that. All I wanted was a little relief, and buying a pair of knock-off or no-name-brand shoes would only make the bullying worse. But she said it was my only option and that I could live with whatever she was going to buy.

Later that afternoon, I went to her closet and found an old pair of white Reeboks she hadn't worn in months. I pulled them out and tried them on. They weren't the best fit, but they had the Reebok logo on the side and weren't immediately recognizable as women's shoes. I asked my mom if I could have them. She said I could if it meant we didn't have to go to Payless. Of course, I agreed to that. I wore those shoes the very next day to school, and the bullying about my worn-out shoes stopped. The kids didn't have a reason to pick on me, and for a while, the fights stopped too.

No matter what was happening at school, Mom still expected the house to be clean to her standards every night when she got home from work. My brother, sister, and I knew this was the expectation, but we also knew her standards were a moving target dependent on her mood. Sometimes the usual cleaning routine was enough. The dishes were done, the counter was clean, the floors were swept and mopped, and she would be satisfied. Other times, this was only scratching the surface.

We got pretty good at guessing her mood by her attitude in the first couple of seconds after she arrived home. One late summer evening, we heard the front door slam against the hallway wall, and we knew it wasn't going to be good.

She immediately started arguing with Buddy. She yelled and demanded to know what he had been doing all day. Had he even left the basement? What had the kids been doing? And then she started in on the cleaning. She went on a tear. Why wasn't the floor under the kitchen table clean? Had anyone cleaned under the radiators? Look at all this dust! What about the corners of the living room?

She yelled for all of us to get into the kitchen, and we formed up in a military line while she tore into us.

The rant started. She was working two jobs to help support all of us, and all she wanted was a clean house when she came home. Was that too much to ask? What did we do all day while she was at work? Why couldn't she count on us, and why weren't we able to complete such a simple task? She didn't ask too much of us, just a clean house so she could rest her feet at the end of the day.

My brother, sister, and I just looked at our feet. We knew that this was not the time to say anything or reply to any of her questions. She kept yelling, and we kept standing, wondering when and how it would end. She went on a while longer, then abruptly stopped and walked out of the kitchen. The three of us looked at each other, wondering what she was doing and trying to figure out whether it was over or if we should continue to stand there in silence.

The front door opened and shut, and we heard her car engine start. The door opened again, and she entered the kitchen with a satisfied look on her face.

"Get in the car," she said through clenched teeth.

We walked out the front door with her following us, no Buddy in sight. I'm guessing the coward had already run back to the basement. We climbed into the running sedan without a word. She started driving without telling us where we were going or why. About halfway there, Phil figured it out and whispered to Sharon and me, "I think she's taking us to Dad's." I looked around and realized he was right. We were on the main route to his house in the suburbs. I couldn't hide my smile.

After my parents' divorce, my father had moved out of the city and remarried. My stepmother, Letha, was a very kind and sweet lady. I loved hanging out with them and my stepsister, Stacey, though I was jealous of their lives, especially Stacey's. My brother, sister, and I had all gone through the trauma of our early lives with my dad on the South Side of Chicago. While I lived in the hood with a molester in my basement, my father and his new family were in the suburbs with good schools and a nice house. I always wondered why I hadn't been a part of this and why Stacey got to live a life that should have been mine.

We pulled into the driveway, and Mom got us out of the car. She walked us up to the front step of my father's house, rang the doorbell, got back into her car, and pulled away without a word. She didn't stay to talk to my father, and she didn't tell us goodbye. She just left us there like she'd dropped off a baby in a basket at the firehouse or a bag of trash on the curb.

My stepmother answered the door. Her usual smile changed to a genuine look of concern when she realized my mom wasn't with us.

"Hey, kids," she said. "What are you doing here?"

Phil spoke up. "Mom dropped us off. She don't want us, so we're here now."

The concern on Letha's face deepened as she tried to figure out what to do or say. After a tense and uncomfortable handful of seconds, she attempted to force a smile and asked us to wait outside for a minute while she got our father. The door shut, and there we stood. Alone again.

I'm not exactly sure how much time went by or what my father and stepmother discussed on the other side of that closed door. Eventually, it opened again and my dad appeared with his coat on. He didn't invite us in, and it was evident he was more annoyed to see us than anything. He looked us over and let out an exasperated sigh. "Come on, kids," he said. "Get in the car."

We piled in and sat in silence as he drove us back to my mom's house. Occasionally, he would glance at the three of us in the rear-view mirror and sigh. Phil tried to talk to him a couple of times but only got one-word answers. It was pretty clear we were a burden he didn't want or at best wasn't prepared for that evening.

I stared out the window and watched the traffic and streetlights stream by. It was getting dark, and all I felt was lonely and worthless. I didn't want to go back to my mom's house with Buddy sitting in the basement, smoking weed, and doing who knew what else. I didn't want to go back to school in the fall and face the bullying and the fights. I didn't want to be afraid anymore. All I wanted was someone to love me.

Sometime before we left his house, Dad or Letha had called the police and asked them to meet us in my mom's driveway. We pulled up to her house, and he told us to stay in the car. The cops were there, and my mom was already talking to them. Dad walked up to my mom and said something we couldn't hear. They started yelling at each other, occasionally pointing at us in the car and yelling even more. The cops more or less watched from the sidelines as my parents were careful not to touch each other while they shouted. Eventually, my dad came back to the car and told us to go in the house.

We slid out of the car and started toward the front door. I walked by my mom. She was furious. The cops were talking to her, and I heard them say we had to stay with her. I caught the officer watching me walk by, and I could see the sadness and pity in his eyes. I ran to my room, climbed into my bed, and covered my head with my pillow. Tears streamed out of the corners of my eyes. More than anything, the tears pissed me off.

Under the pillow, my only thought was that no one wanted me. My mom had driven me to my dad's house because she was so disappointed and so unhappy with me that she no longer wanted me, but my dad wouldn't even let me into his house when I appeared on his doorstep. He could have been upset with Mom for dropping me off unannounced—he likely felt disrespected—but that didn't give him the right not to acknowledge me, or even say hi. Instead, he had punished me and my brother and sister for our mother's failure and had left us feeling even more discarded. Weren't these the people who were supposed to raise me, to make me feel important, safe, and loved? Instead, both of them were willing to just throw me aside like garbage. I felt hopeless and alone. Where else could I go?

chapter 6

Mom and Buddy's relationship seemed to go through phases, and at one point, they actually separated. Money had grown tight because of the loss of Buddy's income. Mom continued to put in extra hours and saved what extra money she could. Sure, life was pretty dark at this point, but occasionally, some light would come through. One such event happened during this time of separation.

Michael Jackson had a concert coming up in Chicago. I had begged for months to be able to go, but Mom countered every time, telling me we just didn't have the money. Plus, how could she take the time off work to take us even if she could afford it?

After being told no about a hundred times, I gave up and came to terms with the fact that I would not be going to the concert. To my complete surprise, Mom came home the week of the show and announced that she had managed to save enough money to get us all tickets. We were going to see Michael Jackson, in person, that Friday night! I thanked her over and over and dreamed about what the show would be like.

In my young mind, the week took forever to pass. Each day dragged on until it was finally Friday morning. I could barely keep still in my chair at school, and when the final bell rang, I ran out of the door to get home as fast as I could. My entire family piled into the car and we headed to the concert. Our seats were way in the back of the auditorium, and Michael looked to be about the size of an ant from our vantage point, but I didn't care. We watched the entire concert on the big screens that had been set up to give us a better view. That night was one of the happiest of my young life.

Shortly after, Mom reconciled with Buddy and he moved back in. My family life continued to worsen with Buddy around. He and Mom would fight off and on about everything from money to his drug use in the basement to how clean the house was. At the same time, my brother was out of the house as much as he could be, and my sister wanted nothing to do with any of us. My mom and brother would get into arguments any time he was home, so he simply stopped showing up.

I, too, began to avoid going home after I started finding my way on the streets. There was no reason to as the fighting between Buddy and my mom grew even more constant. She would come home and start in on him when he didn't know where any of her kids were. I didn't care anymore. My family had abandoned me, at least in my eyes, and without their support and protection there was nowhere safe to turn but the streets.

My gang experience on the South Side of Chicago wasn't like they portray in movies about Southern California. The gangs in my hood didn't control large areas of any part of the city, and there wasn't an initiation process that involved getting jumped by fellow gang members or killing a member of a rival gang. Instead, gangs controlled or operated on a street-by-street basis, and sometimes block-by-block. The Blackstones happened to be the gang that operated on my street.

The gang was founded in the late 1950s in the Woodland neighborhood and grew over the years. Law enforcement in the area still considers it to be one of the most powerful and sophisticated street gangs in Chicago to this day. The colors of the gang are red and black, and the main symbol, the five-pointed star, indicated that the gang members were Brothers or People. There wasn't an elaborate or documented initiation process. One of the easiest ways to show that you were a Blackstone was to wear your hat tilted to the left.

A few streets down were the Gangster Disciples. They were formed on the South Side of Chicago in the late 1960s and use the six-pointed star as their logo. Had my home been a couple of blocks in their direction, I would have been a member of their gang instead. They were the Blackstones' rivals, and they wore their hats to the right.

The reason Buddy didn't know where I was most nights was because I had been hanging out with a couple of new friends. We knew that the Blackstones existed and that they provided a brotherhood, a family, and a sense of belonging that we were missing at home. I saw the gang influence in our neighborhood all the time now. Drug use and prostitution were happening at all hours. It wasn't uncommon to see multiple arrests in a single day or to witness a drive-by shooting. Still, I felt safer with my friends in the streets than I did in the house with Buddy.

I came home later than usual one night and walked through the front door, ignoring both of them as I made my way to the living room. I didn't want to be a part of whatever fight they were having. My brother came home from ball practice shortly after me. He wasn't so lucky and caught the end of my mom's rage. I heard her yell at him about not cleaning the kitchen. He yelled back that he was just getting home which set her off on another tirade about making one of the other kids do it. I heard someone go down to the basement but ignored it.

A few seconds later, the entire house went dark. I jumped off the couch and ran toward the kitchen. I hated the dark. My mom told me to go to the basement, that something must have tripped a circuit breaker and to go flip the switches back on. I started down the stairs, got about halfway down and said, "Hell, no. I won't go." The dark shook me to my core, and I didn't want anything to do with it, so I turned around and came back up. Sharon let out an exasperated sigh and went down the stairs. She didn't know it at the time because of the dark, but she actually walked right by Phil while she was yelling out for him. She came back upstairs, got my mother, and the two of them went down together. I trailed along behind them but decided to stay upstairs.

Next thing, I heard my mom screaming, and then the lights came back on. Sharon had found the switches. I went about halfway down the stairs to see what was going when I heard Sharon scream, "Let her go, let her go, let her go!" My mom screamed again, and I took off up the stairs and to our neighbors, screaming for help the entire way.

By the time I'd gotten back home, my brother had taken off and my mom was back in the kitchen, still breathless but okay. Phil had wrapped a belt from a robe around her neck and was trying to kill her. We didn't see Phil for about a week after that. He had gone to live with a friend and didn't want to come back, but eventually, the family he was staying with told him he had to. I knew something was going on with him. He had never acted out like that before. I couldn't help but wonder if Buddy had gone after him the same way he'd gone after me. He was home even less after that night and spent most of his time with his friends or at practice.

Over the next several months, Sharon started to stand up to Buddy more regularly, and I could see him getting more intimated by her. He would still ask her to come to the basement but he didn't retaliate if she spoke back to him. Don't get me wrong, they'd still get into it, but he was scared of her. One of their fights got so heated while she was ironing that he called her a bitch. She snapped back and threw the iron at him, missing his head by less than an inch. He ducked and retreated to the basement. I smiled, so proud to be her brother in that moment.

Even with Sharon's retaliations, Buddy kept forcing us to watch *Behind the Green Door*. That porno, along with being molested, had taken its toll on my mind. I became depressed, anxious, and incredibly angry. I used to perform during family reunions because I loved the music and I loved being on stage. I felt loved and supported. Now I performed more aggressively and did it for the attention. I was needy, and I had no empathy anymore. On top of it all, I was scared all the time. I was afraid of others taking advantage of me, hurting me, touching me. I had the thought that all gay people must be molesters. How else could I explain what Buddy had done to me?

It dawned on me that all of the times that he was wrestling with me, touching me, and making me rub on him was a sick way of him getting off. Getting what he wanted while taking advantage of me. My adolescent curiosity about sex was driven by this sense of fear about it. I wanted to know more about my situation, and I wanted to know why he had decided to prey on my family and me. It started as a curiosity and quickly grew into an obsession, almost like a virus spreading in my brain.

I wanted to see every female naked, and I would climb up stairwells and up the side of houses to peep into my neighbors' windows. I wanted to see them in the bathroom, in the shower, wherever I could catch a glimpse. I'd drop my pencil in the school hallway on purpose so I could look up girls' skirts as they walked by. For a portion of my life, it became my greatest goal to see as many naked women as I could.

As my mind continued to twist and my thoughts darkened, I came to the conclusion that this was who I was now. I was a product of my situation and I no longer had a choice. My life was going to be full of fear and anger. I didn't deserve real love since no one around me had ever shown me any. The only exception was my grandmother. God, I love her. It was her unconditional love for me that showed me what true love could look like. Unfortunately, she was in Mississippi, and while I knew she loved me, it wasn't much help in my current situation. The street was the only place that provided any sort of reliable family. In my mind, I didn't have a choice, and this was who I was supposed to be.

I grew to hate Buddy more and more with every day that passed. My friends on the street were all turning to the Blackstones. They were having experiences similar to mine—a lack of family support and guidance—but no one talked about it. We just turned to each other and to the only natural support we could find. I was still afraid and wasn't convinced that the gang was what I needed, but I was pushed closer every day.

The tipping point came one afternoon in the fall. I came home from school and Buddy was in a bad mood. We started fighting immediately after I entered the house. He grabbed me by my t-shirt, and I pushed his hands away.

"You can't touch me like that. You're not my father!" I screamed as tears started to fill the corners of my eyes.

His face crinkled and distorted in pain and rage. He pulled back and hit me square in the chest as hard as he could. I stumbled back slightly and he grabbed my shoulder and hit me again in the same spot. Pow! He hit me again and again and again. It felt like he was going to cave my chest in. He hit me one more time, just as hard as the first one.

He looked me right in the eyes. Saliva trickled its way out of his mouth, and he sneered. "I'm on the edge," he shouted. "I'm on the edge, and I'll kill you if I got to."

Pow! Another punch to chest.

I knew I was crying but I didn't say anything. I couldn't. The air had been knocked out of me, and I wasn't sure what to do.

A couple more punches, and he let go of my shirt. He hunched over, trying to catch his breath, but he never took his eyes off me. I don't know if he was expecting me to retaliate or if he was trying to decide if he should keep going. He took a few more breaths, stood up, and retreated back down into the basement.

He became his own virus, and he wasn't strong enough to tackle the infection, so he felt like he had to hurt others. He wanted others to feel his pain. He destroyed our whole family, and I often wonder what our relationship and my life would have been like had he not run into my mom outside that hospital all those years ago. But none of that mattered that fall afternoon. I had been hurt again, and it was the last time I was going to let someone in my own home bring that pain on me. I was done crying, and I was done looking for love and support that would never be there. If this was what the world wanted me to be, I might as well stop fighting it.

I went to my bedroom, wiped the tears from my cheeks, and grabbed my baseball cap off of the table. No more crying, no more fear. I looked in the mirror and pulled the hat down over my head with both hands. As I walked out the front door, I pulled it to the left.

I'd chosen a new family.

I was now in a gang.

I was a Blackstone.

chapter 7

My education continued, and I participated in the graduation
ceremony at my local neighborhood school like any other normal
student. The Chicago public schools used a lottery system to deter-
mine which high school students would attend after this ceremony,
and it wasn't based on neighborhoods or district boundaries like a
lot of other systems. I wanted to go to Julian High School. It was in
my neighborhood, and more importantly, I'd be going to school with
kids from the same gang I was in. One of the other schools in the lottery was Morgan Park. It was in a different neighborhood, and it was
a school run by Gangster Disciples. That was the last place I wanted
to be. The lottery happened, and my fate was sealed—I was heading
to Morgan Park.

It doesn't take long for rival gangs to figure out who's a member
of which gang, and within the first week of school, the GDs knew I
was a Blackstone. I didn't care because I wasn't scared of what they
might do. I knew I had my gang family to back me up and protect
me. It didn't mean I was an idiot though. I wasn't going to walk

through the halls and pick a fight, but I wasn't going to punk out if a fight found me.

I had to ride the CTA buses to school and back because there wasn't a school bus, and I quickly learned that I couldn't get off the bus right in front of the school. There was always a group of gang members waiting to beat me up or try to scare the members of my crew who got off the bus there. I wasn't afraid to fight them, but I also didn't feel the need to instigate fights without a reason. I wasn't one of those hotheaded gangsters who was always looking for trouble or running my mouth. We had those guys, and they were part of the gangster lifestyle, but we also needed some cooler heads or we'd all just end up dead.

I started to vary my routes in order to prevent forming a recognizable pattern. Sometimes I'd get off the bus four stops before the school and walk the rest of the way. Other times, I'd ride it all the way. It let me decide which path to take and which entrance to go to in order to avoid any unnecessary fights. Of course, it didn't always work, and the GDs would catch me on my walk to school or find me eating my lunch in the schoolyard and start a fight.

The last place I expected a fight was the basketball court. It was large and had six different hoops allowing for multiple games to be played at once. The fences were tall to provide some height so the ball couldn't get out but also so players didn't fall out of the court if they were going too hard and couldn't slow down before running into one end or the other. The gate was shorter, but it still had pointed metal tips at the top to keep kids from trying to jump over and wreck the court. They were sharp as hell, and I had seen other kids cut themselves on it doing stupid pranks or trying to show off.

We usually played three-on-three after we finished lunch. I was a track kid in high school, so I was fast, but I could hoop a little bit too. Remember, I was living in Chicago when Jordan was playing with the Bulls, and every young black kid wanted to be like Mike. One afternoon, I was playing with a couple of other kids when I noticed everyone else was starting to leave the court. Lunch wasn't over, and we still had plenty of time to finish our game, but the other guys I was playing with took off. That's when I saw four guys walk through the gate and chain it shut so no one could leave. I knew they were coming after me.

Two of the guys had already started fighting one of the other kids that hadn't made it out before the gate was locked, and the other two were walking toward me. They had these cocky smiles on their faces as they approached. I knew they wanted me to be afraid. It gave them a sense of power. But they were too cocky and left me a running lane to the chained gate. Maybe they didn't think I could make it or I wouldn't try it, but I took off in a full sprint toward the gate and I jumped it like a hurdle; it was like I was a rabbit running from a dog. Nothing touched me, and when I hit the ground, I took off.

I didn't look back, but I could hear them messing with the chains and yelling as they exited the court and followed me. I was fast and knew I could outrun them, but another crowd had already formed, and a couple other guys came out in front of me and stopped me in my tracks. Bo was the first kid to get in my face and start throwing punches. A crowd circled around us leaving me no room for escape. I had to fight him. He was a shorter, light-skinned kid, and I was able to take him easily, but it didn't take long for me to tire.

For those of you who have never been in a fight, it's not like the movies. You don't just keep punching and kicking a guy and never run out of energy or get punched and kicked yourself and just keep fighting like nothing happened. It's draining, and it hurts.

Bo looked around after I'd hit him in the mouth, and a guy named Napoleon shoved him aside and out of the circle. As he pushed him away, I heard him say, "I got this nigga, I'll fight him.

Get out of here."

Napoleon was bigger and scarier than Bo. I didn't want to fight him, but I knew that if I didn't, he'd kick my ass and leave me for dead. Besides, I could see some of my people in the crowd, and I knew they'd have my back if anything got too bad.

Napoleon and I started swinging. We both got in some good hits, and I was kind of impressed with how well I was doing. We kept going around, and I could see Napoleon was starting to get tired too. I made eye contact with one of my brothers, almost pleading for him to jump in, but he just looked away.

A third guy jumped in, and Napoleon backed out. I was exhausted by this point, but I had to keep fighting. I desperately looked around at the crowd again after I landed a good hit on the third guy, trying to find someone to take my place or jump in for me. All of my people were gone except for one guy named Terrell. We locked eyes, and I motioned for him to take my place.

Smack! The third guy hit me right in the face. I stumbled back slightly dazed, but didn't lose my balance. I got my senses back and landed another blow to his gut. He fell back, and I looked back toward Terrell. He was still just standing there looking at me, watching me get my ass kicked. The third kid backed out, and a fourth guy came in. At this point, I was done. I didn't want to fight anyone else. I just wanted out of there. A gap appeared in the circle of students, so I took off and ran as hard as I could until I got back to my neighborhood.

Some of my brothers were sitting on their porches when they saw me run down the street. They came after me, and once I caught my breath, I told them what had happened at the basketball courts. Two guys, Marcel and Andrew, were both pissed that Terrell hadn't done anything at the fight and said we needed to talk to him on his way home after school. He had to walk through our neighborhood to get to his bus stop, and we knew he'd be getting on at 95th and

Throop in front of Longwood Academy.

The Academy was an all-girls school, and classes had just ended as we got on campus, so we did what any high school guys would do in that situation: hit on the girls as they left the building. We didn't get anywhere, but it was better than being shot down by the girls at our normal high school.

Terrell was a big dude. He was a football player and worked out all the time. I wouldn't want to confront him one-on-one, even though he hadn't helped me in the fight, but now I had backup. He passed by us as expected on his way to the bus stop.

"There he goes," I said, loud enough that he could hear me. "Dude watched me get jumped at school and didn't do shit about it."

Marcel clenched his fists and ran over to Terrell. He got right in his face and pushed him against his chest. "How you gonna watch one of your brothers get jumped and you do nothing?"

"What are you talking about?" Terrell said.

"You know what I'm talking about. How you gonna let one of your brothers get jumped and do nothing about it?" Marcel said, a little more aggressively.

Terrell backed up and said, "I don't know what you're talking about. I don't want no trouble."

At this point, Marcel had had enough. He picked Terrell up and slammed him to the ground.

Andrew and I both took a step back, not expecting Marcel to get into it with him right there. I heard Andrew say, "Damn, nigga!" as Marcel hit Terrell again. Then Andrew jumped into the fight.

It didn't make sense because Terrell was so much bigger than Marcel. Maybe Marcel had caught him by surprise, but he kept wailing on him and Terrell kept taking it. Eventually, Terrell took off and Marcel yelled, "Pussy!"

Marcel turned back to me, and he looked pissed. He came up to me and got in my face. "I ain't helping you no more. I ain't fighting for you no more."

"What you talkin' about? I did fight," I said. "Dude, why didn't you tell me you was gonna go fight him? I would have fought him, too, but your ass kicked his ass so fast I didn't have time to step in."

Marcel smiled at that.

The next day at school, I was waiting in line to get lunch, and Terrell walked up to me. I was about to say something about the fight the day before when he punched me right in the eye so hard it almost knocked me out. I remember thinking I should fight back, but I didn't think I could win. I was also so dazed from the force of his punch that I didn't really know what was going on. A couple of kids and a teacher broke us up right away because we were still in school, and we both got sent to the office.

The principal questioned both of us and asked what was going on. I didn't tell them anything because I wasn't a snitch. Everything ended up getting dismissed because neither of us would talk.

The damage to Terrell's reputation had already been done. We all knew now that he wasn't a true gangster. He wasn't someone who would help a brother out no matter what. He just wanted the name, the title, and the recognition of being a Blackstone, but he wasn't a brother, and I would never expect help from him in the future. It also meant I wouldn't help him either. A true brother, a true gangster, didn't need to know the situation or whether they were going to win or lose. All they needed to know was that a brother needed help and they would be there.

I kept riding the city buses because it was the only way for me to get to school and back home. Most of the time, there were kids waiting at the bus stop to fight us if we got off, but one day, instead of waiting outside the bus at the normal stop, four of them got on. I knew they were GDs right away because they had their caps pulled to the right. Mine was pulled to the left, so they knew who I was, too. They surrounded me on all sides, but didn't say anything.

I looked around and recognized one of the four. He was always messing with me at school and running his mouth trying to start a fight. I hated him, but there was nothing I could do on the bus. There was only one of me and four of them. I stared ahead and waited for the next stop, trying to decide whether I could get off the bus without a fight starting.

I decided the best course of action was to run off the bus at the next stop. I was working up my nerve, holding on tight to the seat ahead of me as we approached the curb. To my surprise, three of the four stood up just before I got to my feet. The one that always punked me stayed in his seat. I kept my butt glued to the vinyl, knowing that something would start if I got off the bus with the other three, but they walked down the aisle and got off the bus as a bunch of my guys from the neighborhood got on. I didn't know any of them or what school they had come from, but I saw their hats pulled to the left. I knew this was my chance to finally get back at that punk for all of the harassment he had pulled on me during the school year.

The bus started forward, and I stood up. The kid looked over at me and I looked him right in the eyes and yelled, "Blackstone!" The other brothers who had gotten on at the last stop all stood up and looked at me and yelled in unison, "Blackstone!" These were true gangsters. They knew what it meant to support a brother and be there when someone needed help. Not one of them questioned what I was doing or why I was doing it. They heard the Blackstone call and were ready to do whatever I needed.

I could see the fear behind the kid's gaze as we locked eyes. He was trying to look tough, like he wasn't afraid, but he knew what was coming.

"This nigga is always giving me shit. Always clownin' me and messing with me. His brothers ain't around to help him now, and I think it's time he got what's coming to him," I announced. And with that, I hit him in the mouth.

The other guys jumped in and started kicking and punching him.

"Blackstone, fool!"

"All's well, nigga!"

The bus driver started yelling at us to knock it off, and then the bus came to a sudden stop. He stood up and told the kid we were beating on to get off the bus. We kept harassing him as he ran toward the door.

This is why I joined the gang. Not for the fighting, but for the support. For the family and for the power it gave me. I wasn't afraid because I had my brothers around me, and I knew they would be there when I needed them. My brothers were happy to help me beat up a guy who had been harassing me for months and all I had to do was yell "Blackstone." I wasn't worried about repercussions or what the kid might do to me in the future. All that mattered was that I could give him what he had coming and I had my family supporting me through it.

He got to the door and I yelled, "Nigga, don't you ever get on this bus again!" My brothers yelled back after him as he exited the bus and we showed each other some love. We had won an insignificant battle in the war between the Blackstones and GDs, and we were going to celebrate it.

I felt a light tap on my shoulder and turned to see my sister looking at me. I didn't even know she was on the bus. I'm sure she saw the look of surprise on my face as I wasn't good at hiding stuff like that from her.

"What was that all about? I've never seen you go all crazy like that. Are you okay?" she asked.

I just smiled with my brothers around me. "Don't worry about it," I said. "Your brother has support and that nigga got what was coming to him."

She didn't know what to say and didn't ask me any more questions about it.

I rode that high for a couple of days after jumping the GD. That's what the gang did for me. I didn't have the support at home from my blood family with my mom working all the time and my brother doing his own thing. I wasn't afraid when the gang was around me because there was nothing to be scared of. They gave me power, and nothing could touch me. At least not right away.

The problem with jumping someone was that there were always repercussions. It might not be that same day, or the next day, or even the same week. But eventually, my actions in fighting that kid on the bus would come back to haunt me.

A couple of days after the bus beating, another kid came up to me and told me he wanted to fight me after school. He told me he knew what I had done, and he couldn't let it slide. He was about the same size as me, and I knew I had to fight him. I wasn't scared of him though. I figured I could take him. Plus, after I beat his ass, the GDs would be a little more scared of me, and I'd have more power. I told him I'd see him after school and went on with the rest of my day.

We met after school, and I noticed another kid hanging back on the sidewalk. The gangster came up and started telling me how he was going to whip my ass. I let him run his mouth a little bit, then I hauled off and hit him in the stomach. He fell back a bit to catch his breath, then swung back at me. We traded a few hits. He was stronger than I had given him credit for, but I knew I was going to win. That was until the other kid appeared out of nowhere and hit me upside the head.

I didn't know it at the time, but this gangster had an agreement with the other kid that if I started to whoop him, the kid would tag in. The fight turned from one-on-one to two-on-one, and they quickly overtook me. Each of them traded blows and kicks all over my body, the gangster shouting that I was getting what I deserved. The other kid never said a word, just kept hitting me until the fight was over.

I lay there for a little while before I got up to catch the bus home. My lip was busted, and I had a black eye already starting to form. I could feel the swelling in my head and jaw. I rode the bus home that afternoon with passengers casting sideways glances in my direction, trying to figure out what was going on but not saying anything. My mom got home too late to see what had happened to my face because I was already asleep. The next morning, I left after her, so she never knew about that fight.

I was pissed at the GD and the guy who had jumped me after school, and I wanted nothing more than to get back at them. They jumped me because I had jumped one of theirs. It was my right to jump that kid and teach him a lesson. Most other gangsters would have done just that, continued the cycle. There was no reason to report it to the school or the cops. They couldn't do anything about it anyway because we were all minors. I spent the next couple of days trying to figure out how and where to get back at him.

It may have been the time passing and my emotions calming down, but after those two or three days of planning my retaliation, it hit me. If I jumped him after school, he would get with another couple of his brothers and jump me another time. The cycle would continue on and on with more Blackstones and GDs getting involved. I also realized that no matter what I did, I was still going to the rival gang's school. Eventually, they would catch me by myself, and the next time they did, it could be far more than two of them beating on me.

Being a gangster and being in a gang was my way of earning support and power, but it didn't mean I had to get involved in every fight or retaliation. Deep down, part of me knew I still needed to be smart or things could easily get out of control. Other guys loved fighting, and they would be happy to continue the cycle of retaliation over and over until someone died or went to jail. I wasn't ready for either of those things, and I didn't have that mentality. So I broke the cycle. I didn't retaliate. I was tired, and I didn't want to fight anymore.

That decision probably saved my life. The GDs still ran their mouths, and I still got into fights, but I didn't always escalate things like many of my Blackstone brothers did. Every time I walked away was another moment the cycle couldn't continue and the retaliation couldn't get out of hand. Some might say I wasn't a true gangster because I didn't want to fight all the time or get my revenge when I had every right to. I wanted power, and I didn't want to be afraid, but I also didn't want to die over some gangster looking at me wrong on the bus.

My school and gang life continued much the same after that. There were more fights between the Blackstones and the GDs. I was involved in most of them. There never was a clear winner or loser, just another retaliation. As long as I had my brothers around me, we were invincible. At least that was what I thought. Then the All-Nations picnic happened, and I found myself with a gun to my head.

chapter 8

I woke up in the hospital bed with tubes coming out of my mouth and nose. Rhythmic beeps from the heart monitor and the gentle pulse of the oxygen machine beside my head reminded me just how bad a shape I was in. My left eye was still mostly swollen shut, and my head, ears, and a portion of my face were covered in bandages and gauze. I timidly lifted the sheet covering my chest and upper body only to discover more bandages and stitches where the knife had sunk into my flesh. I tried to say something, but the tube down my throat prevented any noise from escaping my mouth. My eyes darted around the room to see if anyone else was there. The rhythm of the heart monitor picked up when I realized I was alone. Again, I tried to make my voice work, but no words came. The monitor beeped faster, and a nurse walked in.

"It's okay, honey. It's okay," she said as she came to my bed. I knew she could see the fear and uneasiness in my eyes. "You gave us a phone number before you fell asleep, and your dad is already on his way."

My dad? Did she mean my actual dad was coming to the hospital? I didn't remember giving anyone his information, but there was a lot I didn't remember. In fact, the only thing I could recall was the gun pointing at my head and misfiring. I heard the "click" of the hammer again, resounding in my memory, and tried to sit up in my bed, the fear from the street fight rushing over me. But the tug of the tubes laced around my head and the IV in my arm told me I wasn't going anywhere anytime soon. The nurse held my hand and reminded me again that it was okay.

I lay back again and tried to relax, or at least get more comfortable. As I changed positions, I realized I had another tube up my backside. I found out later it was there to search for internal bleeding. A few minutes passed, and the nurse left to check on some other patients in the unit. I was almost asleep when a figure entered my door. I was nervous for my dad to see me in this state but also a little excited that he was the first one to visit me. I knew my mom and siblings couldn't be here yet because they were still in Mississippi visiting my grandma. But those feelings of anxiety and excitement evaporated as Buddy entered my room.

Buddy looked me over and shook his head. I didn't want his pity or his disappointment. I didn't want him in my room at all. Why was he the first one to come? It dawned on me that I had given the staff my mom's phone number, and when they had called our home, Buddy had answered. After all, he was the only one there. He sat down on the couch beside my bed. He didn't say anything, just sat there staring at the other side of the room. I couldn't tell him that I didn't want him there, not with the tube still down my throat, but he knew it by looking at me.

Time moved slowly as we shared the small hospital space together. Eventually, Buddy put his hands on his knees, stood up, and came to the side of my bed.

"I'm not sure what trouble you've gotten yourself into, William. But I did call your mom. Your brother and sister and her are all headed back here. She left your grandma's house as soon as I told her what had happened. I'm guessing they'll be here by tomorrow. I gotta go to work, but your mom's friend, Janet, is on her way to sit with you."

He left without another word. I lay in that bed, by myself, and stared at the white ceiling tiles. Whether he had said it or not didn't matter. He didn't want to be there, and he had more important things to do than sit with his step kid in the hospital while his wife drove more than nineteen hours back home. I was alone again.

The painkillers kicked in, and I fell asleep. I'm not sure how long I was out. When I woke up, Janet was sitting on the couch and holding my hand. My eyes met hers, and I could tell she had been crying. I tried to smile the best I could to let her know I appreciated her being there. She smiled back as a tear ran out of the corner of her eye. Janet stayed and talked to me until my family made it back to Chicago and could get to the hospital. She was there when the nurses removed the tube from my throat, and she helped me take my first drink of water after the ordeal. If I could have hugged her before she left, I would have. For the first time in a long time, I felt the love and compassion I had been longing for.

My family came in together. I was still a little doped up on pain meds, but I was glad they were with me. The swelling in my left eye had already started to go down, but I knew I had to look terrible with the bandages and the medical equipment all around. I caught my brother staring at me. A slight smirk pulled at the corner of my mouth.

"They didn't get me, dawg," I said, though the voice didn't sound like my own. The tube had left my throat dry and raw. I didn't sound like a fifteen-year-old kid; I sounded like a sixty-year-old who had smoked a pack and a half of cigarettes every day of his life. The gravelly voice that emerged surprised me just as it did Phil.

Phil's eyebrows raised, and a look of confusion and anger spread across his face.

"Fool, they got you. What are you talking about?" he asked, still in disbelief at my statement. "What are you talking about?"

"They didn't kill me though. They didn't get me."

Phil was hot now. "Look at your face. Look at your head. Look at you! They got you, man. They *got* you!"

He shook his head and let that final "they got you" trail off. Then he turned and walked out into the hall.

Mom looked me up and down in the hospital bed. She didn't say anything; she just kept staring at me and the machines I was hooked up to. I knew she was disappointed in me, but it wasn't the disappointment I was expecting. Most moms would have been a wreck seeing their kid in a hospital bed. They'd cry over them and say things like, "my poor baby." My mom just stood there looking upset and disappointed. She never said it, but I still wonder if she was more worried about what the neighbors were going to say than if I was truly okay.

My girlfriend came in the next day and tried to comfort me in the hospital bed. She was a wreck, crying and gushing over how she couldn't believe her man was in this condition. She wanted to make me feel better any way she could. I told her there was no way we were going to get anything on with me in that condition.

That afternoon, my dad finally made it in. I was on another round of painkillers, and my conversation with him was a blur. He kept asking me questions. Things like, "Man, what have you gotten yourself into?" and "What are you doing with yourself? What is happening in your life?" Finally I had his attention, and he was willing to listen to me. I broke down in the hospital bed and I told him about the situation at school and in the streets. I explained that people were trying to kill me and that I didn't want to die. I told him how I was scared as hell to go to school every day and walk the streets of our neighborhood.

My dad and I continued to talk, and he asked more about my home life with mom. Any time Mom would come to my hospital room, Dad would leave. Their relationship was so strained by that point, they didn't even want to occupy the same space. By the end of the day, I had told my dad everything and explained that I had to leave or I would end up dead. He wasn't happy about it, but he told me I could move in with him and his family in the suburbs. It wasn't the warm welcome I was hoping for, but it was better than going back to the hood.

The day before I was released, a story on the news caught my attention. I had a small tube television in my room, and it had helped me pass the time during the week and a half that I was in the hospital room. The headline was: "Another drive-by shooting." This wasn't anything new for the South Side of Chicago. It was the location of the shooting that made me pause. A young girl had been shot and killed during the drive-by in the same neighborhood where I had seen Jamal get shot and the GDs had tried to kill me. The news didn't say who had done it, but I knew it had been a retaliation hit by my people for Jamal's death and my beating. In that moment, I didn't care. I was so worried about myself and making sure that I was going to get taken care of that I didn't even feel bad for a little girl's death likely caused by my actions. My only concern was my protection and what other people could do for me. The person I had become was so afraid and so angry that no one else mattered to me. As long as I was okay, it didn't matter who else died or got hurt.

When I was released from the hospital, Mom came and picked me up. The GDs had done a number on my face, and the scars they'd cut into my skin were only starting to heal. The bottom part of both of my ears was gone. My mom didn't know, but I had gotten my ears pierced and only wore earrings on the street when she wasn't around. She hated earrings, so it was something else I kept hidden from her. That didn't matter anymore because some time during the fight they had either been ripped or cut out. I had cuts all over the top of my head, some deeper than others. She looked at me when I climbed into the passenger side of the car, a blank expression on her face.

We got home, and she told me to pack up my stuff. Dad was coming to pick me up that afternoon. I put everything I owned, clothes, shoes, and a couple other random items into a single black garbage bag. Then I sat on my bed, laid the garbage bag at my feet, and looked around my room, occasionally glancing at the bag that contained everything I owned. The only thing I felt was relief—relief that I was getting out of this neighborhood and away from the gang-sters who wanted to kill me. Relief that I was getting out of this house and away from the basement. Relief that I was going to the suburbs and had a chance to start over.

Mom knocked on my door. I looked up at her. She had tears in her eyes. She was sad that I was leaving. She should be sad, I thought. I was her kid, and I was leaving her because of what had happened in the streets, but it still caught me off guard. I wasn't expecting her to actually mourn. If nothing else, I figured she would be as relieved as I was. After all, I had always caused her problems and acted out in school and at home. Without me there, she wouldn't have to worry what the neighbors or the church members thought. She gave me a hug, and I could feel her love for the first time in years. It was weird to finally have some of the love I had longed for my entire childhood the moment I was leaving her.

I walked out the front door to my dad's car. He took the garbage bag from me and told me to get the rest of my stuff. I looked at him, kind of confused.

"This is all I got," I said.

"That's it? That can't be it. Where's the rest of your stuff?" he asked, glancing over my shoulder at the front door of the house.

"That's all I got, Dad. In this garbage bag," I told him again.

He looked upset and a little shocked. It looked like he was trying to figure out if he should ask me one more time or just go look in the house himself. After another pause, he looked at the garbage bag is his hand and back at me, and then let out a long sigh. "Come on, Will. Let's go."

I glanced over my shoulder as I opened the passenger door, taking one more look at my front porch. For some reason, I remember thinking that I would miss that porch and the good times I had on it when I was younger. I sat down, shut the door, and looked over at my dad. He still had a concerned look on his face as he put the car in drive and we pulled out into the street. I stared out the passenger window until the house was gone. As we continued down the highway, the memory of being abandoned by my mother on his front step so many years ago caught me by surprise. I wondered whether this time would be different or if he was taking me in out of obligation.

The sound of my dad clearing his throat shook the thought from my mind. He told me we had to get some more clothes and better shoes. There was no way he was going to have me looking like a bum in front of the kids in his neighborhood. I didn't complain. For the first time in my life, I had name-brand shirts, jeans, and gym shoes. No one could pick on me for how I dressed anymore.

We pulled up to my dad's house later that afternoon, and my stepmom came out to greet us. She gave me a big hug, tight enough to make me wince. I was still in a lot of pain from the first of what would turn out to be multiple surgeries all over my body from the damage of the gang fight. She put her hands on both sides of my face and looked me over.

"Oh, William," she said. "What did they do to you?"

I loved my stepmom and often thought of her as more of a mother figure than my own. She communicated with me and showed her affection. Don't get me wrong, she was tough and didn't take any grief, but she always seemed to understand my pain and my situation.

That night, we had dinner as a family—my dad, Letha, stepsister Stacey, and me. We sat around the table and talked about our day, told stories, and even shared some jokes. It reminded me of those times on the front porch when we had first moved to Washington Heights. In that moment, I felt safe and secure. Later that evening, as I was lying in my bed, I stared up at the ceiling of my new room and rubbed the cuts on my face. I wasn't sure what tomorrow would bring or what my new school would be like, but just then, it didn't matter. I was happier than I had been in a long time.

chapter 9

Over the next several months, I had multiple surgeries on my face, ears, and scalp. The damage done by the GD with the knife wasn't something my body could simply scab over and heal. I developed keloids along my jaw and ears, head and chest. These raised scars continued to be a reminder of the gang fight and a constant source of self-consciousness. Whether or not people were actually staring, it always felt like they were casting sidelong glances at my face and ears.

I got in a lot of fights at my new school, partly due to continued harassment by new kids, and partly due to my desire to be feared and known around the new district. Dad didn't want me sitting around the house when I wasn't in school and thought that football would be a good outlet for the violence I was constantly finding myself in. He told me I needed to try out for the football team and get involved at school. Otherwise, he might as well have left me with my mother.

The football tryouts weren't as hard as I thought they would be, and I made the team. I also started to make some new friends: Brian,

John, Robby, Jason, Harry, and Jerry. They became my crew. They weren't Blackstones, but they had my back and I had theirs. Whatever came up, I knew I could count on them, and they knew they could count on me. It didn't matter whether they'd started the fight or not. I'd jump in and make sure my brothers were taken care of, just as I'd done in the Blackstones.

Football was a good outlet, but it didn't stop the fights. Kids at school started calling me "Tyson" after Mike Tyson. I had a soft voice, and I wasn't afraid to pop a kid in the mouth if they asked for it. I finally started to have some of what I desired back on the South Side of Chicago. People were scared of me. They didn't know what I might do, and anyone who challenged me either got taken down or made to feel terrified. I didn't win every fight I got into, but I made sure that everyone who wanted to fight me wouldn't forget the experience.

There was a skating rink on the school grounds, and it was a favorite hangout for wannabe gangsters. These guys liked to mess with me, and one afternoon they challenged me to a fight. They kept running their mouths, telling me I was a nobody and they weren't afraid of me. I had a couple of my crew with me, and we started fighting. I'm not sure how many people ended up getting in the middle of that brawl. I just knew that I was hitting kids right and left, and occasionally, someone would get a good hit on me.

It ended up being one of the bigger fights I'd been in since moving in with my dad. I'm still not sure how I ended up getting out of it as clean as I did, but when it was over, I knew that this was an opportunity I couldn't waste. Kids starting running off while others just lay around looking at each other, and there I was in the middle of it. I smiled at one of the mouthy kids who'd started everything and started singing a Michael Jackson song. Then I just walked away singing as loud as I could.

Each step I took and every note I sang had more people looking at me. They couldn't hide the concern from their faces. Each and every person I passed looked at me like I was a lunatic. I could hear whispers coming from groups of onlookers, kids who had seen the fight but hadn't participated in it.

"What's wrong with that nigga?"

"Why's he singing? Is he crazy?"

"Man, I don't know. Let's get out of here!"

I loved it. There I was in the middle of the suburbs, and all these kids thought I was nuts because I was singing after a fight. Even though I wasn't on the South Side anymore, I was still a Blackstone at heart, and I knew these kids, even those in my own crew, would never be able to understand what I'd gone through before moving out here. That fight was probably one of the craziest things they had ever seen. To me, it was normal. And the fact that they thought the singing made me even crazier was a bonus.

The school talent show was only a couple of months after the fight at the skating rink. One of my crew had heard me singing after the fight and had told the others that I had a voice. They'd make me sing every now and then, whenever a new pop song came out or when there was a really good R&B hit on the radio. A few weeks before the show, one of them came up to me and told me that I needed to be in the show, that he wanted me to sing.

I laughed in his face. "Man, I'm not getting in no talent show. I'm a thug, fool," I said with a chuckle.

"Man, cut that thug shit out, we all know you can sing, Will," he said.

I told him no again and to drop it. He just shook his head and walked away. For me, the discussion was over. I was a gangster, and I wasn't going on stage to sing for anyone.

The day of the talent show came, and I agreed to go watch it with my boys. The stage was set in the lunchroom auditorium, and there were kids from all over the area watching. We cheered for the good acts and made fun of the bad acts along with everyone else. The show was coming to a close when the announcer called out the next act.

"For our next performance, please welcome William Holmes!"

There was an audible gasp from the audience, which might have been just me trying to figure out what the hell was going on. My first thought was, "Is there another William Holmes around here?" I looked around, trying to figure out who this other kid was. My friends looked at me and said, "They're talking about *you*, fool." Then they grabbed my shoulders and half-pushed and half-pulled me up onto the stage.

"Y'all didn't just sign me up for this talent show!" I yelled. "You motherfuckers didn't just put me in this talent show."

They laughed and called at me to get up there, forcing me up the stairs until I was in the middle of the stage. The lights all focused on me along with about six hundred eyes. I could see the confusion on their faces. The thoughts they must be having right now: "What's he going to do, and why is he on that stage? What is Tyson about to do?"

I pulled my hat down over my face to hide from everyone. I was nervous and pissed that I was even up there. My mind started racing with ways to get out of the situation and what I was going to do to the guys who'd signed me up for this stupid talent show. It hit me that there wasn't music—no accompaniment. I was going to have to do this acapella or leave the stage a total embarrassment. What was I going to do? The silence from the crowd was deafening, and I could hear a couple kids start booing. Someone coughed. Then a new thought entered my mind. "Fuck it. I'm up here. Let's do this."

I put my head down and let the first couple of notes flow from my throat. Stevie Wonder's "Lately" was one of my favorite songs, and I knew it by heart. If nothing else, I'd sing through the chorus and get off the stage. I heard people start screaming, but I was too nervous to lift my head or take my hat off, which was hiding my eyes. In the darkness, I was safe and secure. The lyrics start, "Lately I have had the strangest feeling, with no vivid reason here to find." The screaming got louder. My only thought was there better not be a fight starting, not while I'm up here singing in front of all of you. "If the thought of losing you's been hanging, round my mind... ooooh." More screaming, and it hit me that it wasn't the noise of a fight breaking out. It was a shout of pleasure, like what I would hear on recordings of Jodeci, one of the hottest groups at the time.

The screaming got louder, and I just couldn't help myself anymore. I had to know what was going on beyond the shadow of my hat. As I slowly lifted my hat up and raised my head, I couldn't believe my eyes. There, in the front row, were at least twenty-five girls looking up at me with big googly eyes. They were in a trance waiting for me to keep singing. I continued on with the song, the run of notes getting easier as I felt their energy. They screamed louder since they could now see my face, and I caught a feeling I hadn't felt since I was singing Michael Jackson in my Spider-Man pajamas so many years ago—joy. I felt joy in the moment. The music and the crowd and the frenzy overtook me, and I was happy.

The shouting continued, and I started to take off my shirt. That sent most of the front row over the edge and girls literally started rushing the stage. Somewhere in the auditorium, I heard one of the administrators shout, "We gotta get this guy off stage!" I kept going, not wanting the moment to end. More screams, more notes, and then everything went black, and my mic went dead. The bastards shut down my entire show!

Looking back, my friends had no idea how much signing me up for that talent show would change the direction of my life. That day, I took a step toward the man I was supposed to be. My love for music and my confidence started to return. The Will that I had tried to bury for the last decade had started to resurface. No matter what had happened to me up to that point, a piece of the true me was still there, wanting to break out and be seen, the part that wanted to be a performer, do some good, and help others who wanted to be heard. And I was ready to listen. But with every step forward, there are bound to be some steps back.

I found out that day that there was power in my voice and that I could use it to get what I wanted. At first, it was just girls. They started coming after me when they heard me sing. Girls way out of my league now wanted to talk to me, date me, sleep with me. Who was I to say no? The continued fighting distracted me along with the new interest of the ladies all around me, and my grades started to slip. My dad didn't like that or the fact that I was dating white girls. Tensions started to rise in my new home.

The attention became a drug to me. I needed more and more to satisfy that original high I felt on the stage of the talent show. There was nothing that could quench the thirst of the monster growing inside of me. I was willing to risk everything I had going for me in the suburbs. It didn't matter that my new family life was starting to unravel, and I could see the distrust in their eyes. I needed the love and admiration of my peers more than anything else, even more than the trust of my dad and stepmom.

My reputation of being a fighter and loose cannon continued to grow in high school. Other guys started testing me and challenging me to prove they were tougher or meaner or more thug than I was. Some of the times it was a legitimate challenge, but other times they just made up stories to get under my skin or provoke a fight.

One afternoon my junior year, a girl I knew told her boyfriend that I had called her a bitch by the lockers. I hadn't, but that didn't matter. He was big, a lot bigger than me, and he was looking for a reason to fight.

"Will, you called my girl a bitch," he said as he pulled back and took a swing at me.

I didn't have a chance to tell him he was out of his mind, and that I had never said a word to her. Before I knew it, I had popped him in the mouth and he was on the ground. I jumped on top of him and started strangling him. For some reason, this poor sap had brought out all of my anger and resentment toward everything that had happened in my life. Everything I had bottled up, I took out on him. His girl started to beat on me with her school folders, but I kept wailing on him. The fight got broken up by some teachers, but things were clear to most of the student body. If people weren't afraid of me before, they were now.

I'd yell, "Pow!" when I hit people, like you see in comic books. This only added to my reputation for being crazy and wild. Soon, kids from other schools were showing up to challenge me on my home turf. Sometimes they would want to fight on school grounds; other times they'd challenge me to fight somewhere else. Eventually, I couldn't even go to a party on the weekends without someone getting in my face to prove they were thug. Of course, that didn't stop me from going out, especially if there were new girls I could impress.

Brian called and told me there was a house party he and a couple other guys from our crew were going to hit up. He invited me along. Something in my gut told me that it was a bad idea, but I decided to go anyway. The party was in a neighborhood I hadn't been to before and would hopefully provide a getaway from all the fighting and everything else going on in my life.

We walked in the front door and saw some other kids from one of our rival schools. They didn't know who we were, but I knew them, and it was pretty obvious they were already drunk. A big guy I had never seen before walked up to our group and started messing with us, wanting to know who we were, why we were in the house, and why we thought we belonged there. I could already feel my temper flaring, and I knew we'd be in trouble if we got into a fight here. We were outnumbered and outside our neighborhood. Who knew whose side the rest of the guys in this room would be on? I grabbed Brian and told him we didn't have to deal with this, that there were other parties we could go to. He agreed, and we headed for the door.

On the way to the car, the big guy caught up with us and got in Brian's face. He started harassing him, calling him a pussy, and trying to get him to fight. I'd had it with that fool by then, so I intervened and got between him and Brian. I could feel the anger, and I knew I could beat his ass. He looked me dead in the eyes, and I saw some craziness there I wasn't expecting. He half spit as he said, "Man, if you don't get out of my face, I'm gonna kill you." I stumbled back as the memory of Buddy and his rage flashed through my mind. I felt his blows to my chest and saw his distorted face with the spit in the corner of his mouth. I looked back over my shoulder at Brian. He was standing there, waiting for me to throw a punch, ready to jump in and swing on this guy. I turned back to my challenger, but he was still waiting to see what I was going to do. So I turned around and headed toward the car.

I heard Brian and the guys from our crew ask me in half-whispers what I was doing, telling me we had to go back and fight. They were angry and disappointed. They'd never seen me turn down a fight and didn't understand why I was walking away from this one. I had almost reached the car when someone, I'm not sure who, hit me in the back of the head. My anger rose, and I forgot for one moment the clarity I had just had. There was a bat in the back seat of the car. I reached through the window and grabbed it. My crew got visibly excited as they saw me turn with the bat in my hand and look up at the big guy who'd started all of this. They knew what was coming next.

"If you swing that bat, I'm gonna kill you, nigga," he said.

Buddy's face was back in my mind along with all the other memories, and I dropped my shoulders and lowered the bat. The big guy had had enough and pulled back his arm to swing at me, but he missed. Someone else from his crew jumped in, wanting to join in on the fight. I started to panic, realizing what was about to go down if I didn't get us out of there. I jumped into the back seat on the driver's side and told my crew to get in. They were already getting surrounded as the big guy's crew joined in on the fight. Brian and the others looked back at me, half fearful and half disgusted after witnessing me back down from a fight we didn't start.

"Get in the fucking car!" I screamed at them.

I didn't want to fight that night. I knew that if I did, one of us was going to die. There were at least seven of them and only four of us. The big guy was serious when he had said he would kill me. I'd seen that look before and knew what it meant for all of us. Sure, we might have been able to fight him and some of his friends off, but one of my crew was going to get seriously hurt if I didn't walk away, and I couldn't have that on my conscience.

They all got into the car, and we took off.

"What the fuck, Will?"

"Why'd you punk out? You never punk out."

"We could have taken those niggas, especially with that bat."

"What's wrong with you?"

I knew they were upset and didn't understand why I was the one who'd decided to walk away. I was always up for a fight. No one got in my face and walked away, at least not in my crew's eyes. They thought I didn't care about anything, especially physical fights, but they hadn't lived through the things I had. I didn't want that to be the day one of us died.

That night defined who I was for them. They thought I was no longer the thug who never backed down, but they had no idea what was going on in my head or in my soul—the moments and thoughts I was reliving as they pelted me with questions on the way home. For most of the drive back, I sat in silence and just took it. How could I explain to them what I had been through and what I had seen in that guy's eyes that told me to leave the party? How could I convince them that I knew one of us would die if we fought? There was nothing I could say or do. So I continued sitting in silence, grateful they were still alive and that I would wake up in the morning.

chapter 10

As my senior year began, one of my teachers called me into her office and explained that if I didn't get passing grades for the rest of the year, I wouldn't graduate. Without these final seven credits, I would have to come back for summer school or attend one final semester in the fall. I told her that if she thought I was coming back for another year, she was out of her damn mind. I was going to get the seven credits and graduate on time. She should have known that if someone told me I couldn't do something, I would do everything in my power to prove them wrong. I finished my senior year with straight As and got all the credits I needed. I was a high school graduate, and needed to figure out what to do next.

One of my family members was an administrator at Western Illinois University. He suggested I apply there and start college if I got accepted. I didn't know the first thing about applying for college, so he walked me through the process and helped me get signed up for the ACT. He told me I needed to study and get a decent score if I wanted to get accepted. I didn't listen, got a score of 17, and still got in.

That summer, I spent a good amount of time working at whatever jobs I could find to build up some cash for school. The summer flew by as I spent my days at work and my nights at various parties. Before I knew it, June and July had passed and August was almost over. The night before I left my father's house and moved into my dorm, I was lying in bed when it dawned on me that the next day I was officially going to be on my own. It was on me to decide what happened next, and I was in control of what I was going to do for the rest of my life. My dad and stepmom dropped me off at my dorm the next morning, helped me unload the possessions I decided to bring with me, and pulled away.

I met my roommate, Rob, later that afternoon. He didn't talk much, and it was pretty clear we weren't going to get along. I never pushed him or got into any fights with him, but a week later, he requested a transfer and moved out. He told me he just didn't see himself living with me for a whole semester. Having an entire room to myself my freshman year of college wasn't the worst thing that ever happened, but it wasn't the best either. I had free range now when I wasn't at class. No one monitored anything I did which meant I could party and have girls over whenever I wanted.

It probably won't surprise anyone who truly knows me to find out that I wasn't college material. I likely knew that before I'd even taken the ACT, but I wanted to experience it. My brother had moved out to Des Moines, Iowa, after graduating high school and had gone to Drake University. He told me stories about his experiences at college, and I didn't want to miss out. I can tell you, I definitely didn't miss out on partying.

Don't get me wrong; I gave it a shot. I signed up for and studied my passion, music. The courses that really caught my attention were those around music therapy. I could have been the first black music therapy teacher in all of America if I would have seen it through. But there was always a distraction, especially with all the ladies around.

These girls were just like me, free and on their own for the first time in their lives. I couldn't help it that they were drawn to my voice. With the scars on my face, some of them thought I was cute, but a lot of them thought I was disgusting. On top of it, I had my own room, so I never worried about getting caught by someone else walking in. Throw in the easy access to booze, and my first year of college was one I would really rather forget.

The first time I got really drunk in my life was on Mad Dog 20/20. I drank it like Kool-Aid when it was handed to me. I was so messed up that I'm not even sure how I got back to my dorm room. Then I had the idea that it would be better if I got naked, so I stripped down and started walking through the dorm hallways. People usually had their doors open on the weekends. It let other students know they were around and was an open invitation for people to drop by their rooms. I started dancing down my hallway buck naked and jumped into every open doorway. Each got their own show as I danced around and sang for anyone who didn't close their door soon enough. Other students heard the commotion I was making and stuck their heads out. A few of them laughed, and the next thing I knew, all the doors on my floor were closed. I guess they didn't appreciate my show.

I went to the bathroom and ended up passing out back in my room. My head was pounding the next morning when I finally woke up. After I climbed out of bed, I found my clothes lying in a heap in the corner. My brain played back some of the previous night, and I laughed out loud as I got dressed. The laughter was short-lived when I came to the realization that all of the cash I'd had the night before was gone. Someone had taken it during my drunken episode.

Between the girls and the partying was the occasional class. I went when I felt like it and did try to apply myself in the music courses. The professors were all old-school in my eighteen-year-old mind and were trying to teach me things I didn't need to know. One of the requirements was that I learn piano. Why would I need to be able to play piano? I could already sing and didn't have any need for what they were trying to teach me. My singing professor was even worse. He wanted me to use my diaphragm. At the time, I didn't even know what that meant. He kept having me do scales and other exercises to teach me proper technique. Why would I need this? I could sing already, and the girls all loved it. I didn't have time for the nonsense he was trying to teach me.

I ended up failing the music lessons and choir because I didn't show up. I was so confident in my own abilities and the success that I had already earned that it didn't make sense to waste my time on what the professors wanted me to learn. They weren't teaching me anything that was going to help me anyway.

One of the bright spots of that first year of college was the creation of my first musical group, Conversion. I got together with three other guys, and we started singing together. One of our first shows was for the college talent show. We sang R. Kelly's "Dedicated" and tore the place apart. The girls were going crazy, almost like they'd done at my solo show in high school. We ended up winning the competition and started singing outside of campus. It was my first time getting paid to sing, and I loved it.

Our group was approached by a lady who wanted to manage us and help us get more shows. We were young and naïve and had no idea how the music industry worked. All we heard was that this woman saw something in us and wanted to help. We signed with her, and she came through, getting us gigs all over the city. She even helped us write and produce our first original song. Everything seemed to be falling into place.

There was a big show coming up, and I was putting off everything to practice with my group. I didn't go to school and didn't work, just put all of my focus on our set and making the most of this opportunity. Our manager told us that if this went well, she could really see our careers taking off. The set built up to our cover of "Freak Me" by Silk. I had the high tenor part, and I was nailing it in our practices. The runs were flawless—each note crystal clear. I knew that if I could pull this off, people around campus would be talking about me for months.

The night of the show came. I was nervous in a good way, with the kind of energy that only comes when you're about to do something big. We'd put in the time, and we had our set on lock. Our final practice the day before had been perfect, and I had no reason to think it would be any different in front of the crowd. The lights went down and we took the stage. I could feel my stomach twist in anticipation. My palms started to sweat. I was on edge and ready to show these people what I could do. The lights came up and the crowd started to cheer before a note had even been sung. It was our time.

To say we were on fire would be an understatement. All of the time spent practicing together was paying off. We hit every note of every song, and the crowd was going nuts. It was unlike anything I had ever experienced on stage. The set continued, each song building on the prior one. The intro to "Freak Me" started, and the girls in the front row lost their damn minds. They knew the song, and they knew I was going to be singing the high part. Everything was coming together better than I could ever have expected.

The song continued and built to the climax. We were all in sync, the harmonies were perfect, and our moves were smooth. We got to the line, "Baby, don't stop," and the group turned to me to show the audience where to look as I started the lyric run. I saw a woman in the front row singing along. She made eye contact with me and knew what was coming. Her arms went up, and she was ready to scream and applaud. I went for the line, confident that I had the ability and the talent. My hand tightened on the microphone, and I took a breath. My mouth opened, but the notes didn't come out. My throat tightened, and my jaw clenched as my voice cracked.

The silence was almost deafening. I took a breath and tried again, but again my voice cracked. One more time, I took a deep breath, grabbed the mic. My mind told my voice that I was going to make this happen. I couldn't let my group down. Everyone was looking at me. I could feel the heat from the lights, and I tried one last time to get through the lyric. My voice cracked again, and I knew I was done. My shoulders slumped. I heard some gasps of shock and disbelief from the audience. Tears filled my eyes as I left the stage in that overwhelming silence. The other three guys finished the set as I sat in the wing, crying, too embarrassed to go back out and face the audience.

Turns out I was the talk of campus for a couple of months, but not for the reason I wanted to be. People talked about the show and made fun of my voice cracking—to my face and behind my back. I felt like trash, like I had disappointed everyone, and my confidence was shattered. I had worked for years to get my groove back, and it was gone in a single, embarrassing night.

Thankfully, the guys in Conversion had my back and encouraged me to keep singing. They rallied around me and got me back on stage, but things were never the same. I was nervous to sing and always afraid that my voice was going to crack again or that I was going to mess something up. We continued to get shows, but our manager wasn't as active and wasn't working as hard for us anymore. It was pretty clear that she had moved on.

Life has a way of teaching you lessons whether you want to learn them or not. Looking back, had I learned proper technique from my music teacher and paid attention to his advice on singing from my diaphragm, I would have nailed my solo. I know now that I was singing so much from my throat that I was wearing it raw, and like working any muscle too much, it had given up. I pushed it too far the night of the show, and it was exhausted. Without that mistake, our manager would have continued to plug our group, and other shows would have happened. Who knows what would have come next?

I could dwell on the past and get stuck there. A lot of great things could have happened, but that door had closed. Other doors were going to open, and other opportunities would come up. I started to take my art more seriously and started to listen to my teachers. Music was it for me. It was all I wanted to do. My other grades suffered, and I ended up getting mostly Ds and Fs in everything that wasn't related to music.

We did other shows, and I started to rebuild the confidence that had shattered on stage. Soon enough, the student body moved on to the next piece of drama, and the talk about my performance subsided. The girls never really quit giving me attention because they knew I had a voice. One girl in particular, Jesse, started to pay me a lot of attention.

It all started when I noticed she was following me to class. I ignored her and went on with my morning. Then I saw her staring at me at lunch. After that, she followed me to the next class and was there after I got out. She followed me to the class after that, too, and that was when I confronted her because I knew it wasn't a coincidence anymore. I spun around to talk to her and stopped dead, taken aback by how beautiful she was. Her long, dark hair was in a ponytail that accented her deep, brown eyes. She was Italian with dark, tanned skin and slim but very thick at the waist. I knew then and there that I wanted her.

I gathered my thoughts and asked her what she was doing. Why was she following me everywhere? She told me she'd heard me singing in my dorm the other day. Her cheeks turned a little pink as she flushed with embarrassment but continued sharing that she loved my voice.

"I've never done this before," she said. "But I'd really like to get to know you more. Anyone who can sing like that…" She trailed off. I smiled and told of her of course we could talk more. Who was I to tell a pretty girl no?

We started dating, and our relationship started smoothly. She was a lot of fun, and I had a good time with her, but she really liked to drink. It was pretty evident that being in college was her first taste of freedom, too, and she was taking advantage of the free-flowing booze. When she drank, she got really sexual. Now, that wasn't a bad thing in the beginning, but it also got exhausting. Not only did she like to party, she also ran her mouth after a few too many. She was drinking weeknights and weekends and started dragging me into her drama.

Guys were always hitting on her and trying to pick her up. She started telling me stories about the guys in the bars to make me jealous. The stories got worse toward the end of our relationship. She came to my room really drunk one night, crying and telling me that I needed to go the bar and beat up a guy there. I got her calmed down a little and asked her what was going on.

"There was a guy at the bar. Says he knows you and doesn't understand why I'm running around with you. Told me I was wasting my time messing around with the dude with scars all over his face. Asked me why I liked you and told me to leave you." She broke into tears again and passed out a little later.

I knew the guy she was talking about but knew it wouldn't be a good scene to go to the bar on my own while he likely had friends with him. Plus, he was on the football team and was huge. I wasn't even sure I wanted to fight him. So I waited a couple of days and confronted him on campus when there wasn't anyone else around. He denied it and told me that she had made the whole thing up. I'm glad I didn't push it any further with him because he ended up being one of the best safeties in the NFL—Rodney Harrison.

Jesse and I broke up shortly after that. I didn't want to keep dealing with her drunken drama and wasn't into her anymore. It wouldn't surprise me if she and Rodney had hooked up after we split.

My freshman year ended, and after talking with my dad about my options for the summer, I decided to move to Des Moines to stay with Phil. He had a place in Clive, one of the suburbs, with an extra room. The plan was to get a job, make some extra cash, and build up some savings. It also gave me an opportunity to try building a relationship with him. He had taken off as soon as he could after graduating high school, and I wanted an opportunity to get to know him. I also hoped he wanted to get to know me a little more now that I was an adult and not just his kid brother anymore. We had a good summer and we were cool with each other, but we never bonded like I hoped we would.

Summer ended, and I started my sophomore year, but I was on academic probation due to my poor grades. I kept going to my music classes but didn't really care about any of the others. That semester ended with me failing most of my classes and not being able to enroll in the winter. My roommate liked me and told me he didn't care if I stayed with him instead of going home, so I stayed for the rest of the year even though I wasn't in school.

I drank and partied my way through the rest of that year fully expecting to move back to my dad's place when summer break came. But he had other plans and told me I wasn't allowed to come back. He had received a copy of my transcripts and knew I wasn't in class anymore. He also knew that I had failed most of the classes I had taken and wasn't going to spend any more money on my education if I was just going to mess it up. There wasn't much else I could do, so I called my mom.

During my freshman year of college, her and Buddy had separated and later divorced. My molester was no longer living in the house, and the basement was open. It did mean that I was moving back to the hood and back to the gang life that I had mostly left behind, but at the time, it felt like I didn't have another choice. I didn't have a job or any savings, and my dad had told me I was no longer welcome in his house. Mom said I could move back in, so I packed up my stuff to head back to the South Side of Chicago.

chapter 11

It had been almost five years since the gun at my head had misfired twice and the Gangster Disciples had cut up my face and body and left me for dead. A lot of things had changed in my life during that time. New relationships had come and gone, and I had learned a lot about who I was becoming, but through it all, both the emotional and physical scars from that day remained. And my mom was basically the same person she'd been the day I'd left her house and moved in with my dad.

She was still working multiple jobs even though all of her kids were out of the house. She was never home. The kitchen was bare because she never brought home groceries. It was pretty clear very early on that she was letting me live there, but that was it. Other than the roof over my head, no additional support would be given. I wasn't afraid to get a job and work, but it would have been nice to try building a relationship with her. It seemed that wasn't an option.

There was a Popeye's close to my mom's home in the Blackstone neighborhood. They needed help and I needed a job. Was it my dream job? No. But it paid my bills, left me some extra spending money, and bought me food. My manager liked me, and I was quickly promoted to a cooking position. Life was pretty smooth, and I was actually starting to enjoy the work.

We split shifts with a bigger crew around the lunch and the dinner rushes. I didn't care which shift I worked, so week to week, my manger just put me in wherever she needed me. There wasn't a back entrance, which required all the employees to come through the main door and go to the back to change and get ready for their shift. We'd have to walk through the main cashier area to get to the back so everyone standing in line could see when employees were starting their shifts and other employees were ending theirs.

I came in for what was becoming my normal shift on Wednesday afternoon. The place was packed and much busier than usual. I smiled at the customers in line. A couple of them returned my smile, but others started to stare and notice the scars and keloids on my face and head. I could feel their eyes still on me as I walked past the cashiers and nodded to my coworkers. It was pretty evident they had been busy for a while from the stress behind their forced smiles. I hurried to the back so I could change into my apron and get on the line to help relieve some of the pressure, but I couldn't get the customers' judgmental and disgusted facial expressions out of my head.

People staring and pointing at the scars wasn't anything new. It happened almost daily and was something that I had mostly learned to live with, but it never got easier. I finished changing and started back toward the kitchen. There was a mirror in the hallway. Most of the time I walked by it, but the customers' looks of unease and disgust were still playing in my mind. I stopped at the mirror and looked at my reflection. The scars were still there, and the keloids had gotten larger. I'd likely need another surgery to shrink them again, but I didn't look too bad. I forced a fake smile and walked into the kitchen.

It was incredibly quiet. No one was cooking anything. There weren't any orders hanging in the window, and a couple coworkers had gone on break. I poked my head out to see what the dining room looked like and was shocked to find it completely empty. This didn't make any sense. Less than three minutes ago, there had been more than a dozen customers waiting in line. Where had everyone gone?

Confused, I went to my manager and asked what had happened. She told me that after I had gone to the back to change, one of the women in line came to the register and asked if I was going to be the one cooking the food. The cashier told her that I was one of the cooks so it was possible that I would be the one cooking her meal. The lady then asked to speak with the manager. The customer asked my manager the same question and was told yes, that I would likely be the one cooking her food. The lady had started a scene and had yelled loud enough for everyone in line to hear, "Oh, hell no. I'm not gonna eat no food cooked by him." She grabbed her kids and left, telling everyone else in line that I was the cook and asking them if they really wanted me to cook their food. One by one, everyone else in line left without ordering anything.

My manager told me she was sorry and walked away. I felt defeated. Did I really look that disgusting that people didn't want the cheap, fried, fast food that I made? I turned and headed back toward the kitchen, looking in the mirror again. There were tears in the corners of my eyes. The only other time I had been more embarrassed was when my voice had cracked on stage. What was wrong with me?

The shift went on without another incident. I stayed in the back where no one could see me, and customers started to come in at a somewhat normal pace. Other than the twelve or so who had initially seen me when I'd first come in, no one else said anything. My shift ended, and I changed out of my apron to head home. A couple coworkers told me not worry about it and invited me to go out for drinks if I wanted to. All I really wanted was to go home and not have these scars on my face anymore.

I had Friday off and decided to go in and get some free food. It was one of the perks of working there. I'm not sure if it was an actual perk or just something the manager let us do. Regardless, all of us got free food when we came in on our days off. My manager was standing behind the cashier line talking with a couple of my coworkers. I walked up and asked the guy working the register for a three-piece chicken. He didn't ring anything up and turned to get me the chicken off the line, but my manager stopped him in his tracks.

"What are you doing? You need to ring up his order," she said.

He looked at her slightly confused and turned to look at me. I didn't say anything. He shrugged his shoulders and went to ring in the three-piece.

"Wait a minute," I said. "What's going on? I work here. We get free food. We've always gotten free food. You told me when I was hired this is something we did here."

She looked me right in the eyes and told me that wasn't a policy and that I had to pay for whatever I was ordering. If I wasn't going to pay, I could leave. I looked back at my coworker, and he glanced toward the floor. Everyone else was also avoiding my eyes, so I turned back to my manager, still confused, and tried to figure what was going on.

In frustration, I finally blurted out, "This shit is crazy! I can't get a three-piece?"

This was exactly what she wanted. Without missing a beat, she told me I was fired. Shocked, I asked her why.

"You're in here demanding free food, and now you're talking back to me, Will. You're fired. Don't worry about your shifts. We'll get it covered."

I left. What else could I do? She had made up her mind, and there wasn't anything I could do to change it. I went home and tried to figure out how I was going to tell my mom I had been fired from Popeye's of all places. What was she going to say? I really didn't want to see her face. I didn't want to see the disappointment that would be there along with the line of questions about why I kept messing up. I was so tired of hearing people say they were disappointed in me. It was a constant reminder that I couldn't do anything right, when all I ever wanted was just to do something right.

She was working a double, so it would be a while before she got home. I was working on my story when I heard on a knock on the front door. It was a weird time for someone to be randomly knocking. I was back in the hood, so I approached the door with caution and looked through the curtain. It was my coworker who had been working the register when I had come in for the chicken.

"What do you want?" I asked as I opened the door.

"You got a bad break there, Will," he said. "She didn't fire you because of the free food thing. We still get free food. She fired you because customers started complaining about your scars. They told her they didn't want to eat the food you were serving. She was looking for any reason to fire you and used the free food thing as an excuse. Sorry, Will. I just thought you should know."

I thanked him but wanted to punch him in the face at the same time. He left, and I closed the door behind him. I was broken. I dropped to the floor and cried. I drowned in all of the negative thoughts that flooded my mind. Was I really that hideous? If I couldn't get and keep a job at Popeye's, could I ever keep a job anywhere? Would anyone ever give me a fair shot, or was this my life now? I managed to get to bed and fall asleep still thinking about the customers' faces and everyone who had ever given me a sideways glance because of my scars.

Mom was home the next morning. I told her my situation. She

asked what had happened, and I told her what my coworker had told me. She nodded her head, but I could tell she didn't believe me. No matter what the circumstances were, she never had my back and always thought there was more to the story, something I wasn't telling her.

I got pretty depressed over the next couple of days staying at home. It was hard to get motivated to look for another job when I had just been fired from one because of my looks. The days crept by, and I wasn't getting any support or love from my mom. All I wanted was some compassion. She had no idea what I was going through every day in that house and neighborhood, all of the pressure and the threats that were my everyday life. Coupled with the scars and harassment, some days it seemed almost impossible to get out of bed. But none of that mattered to her.

I managed to find an escape in my music. It was the constant that brought me both the attention I was seeking and an outlet for all the anger and rejection I felt. Singing let me express myself in a way I wasn't able to with words or actions. It also brought me a peace and calm that was hard to find in the world I now lived in. I sang whenever I had the opportunity—alone in my room, walking down the street, and most often on the bus. That's where I met Stefon.

I rode the CTA daily and usually kept to myself. My Walkman let me listen to the music I wanted and sing along in my head or out loud, depending on my mood. Most people on the bus knew me because we were all regular passengers. They left me alone even if I bugged them with my singing. The route was a pretty quiet one as none of the other passengers really spoke to one another or said anything. Most of the time, the bus was full of people heading to or coming home from work. The afternoon Stefon got on the bus was no different until he boarded.

My normal seat was in the middle of the bus. Stefon walked by and took a seat a few rows back. I had my head down and was humming along to some R&B song. I didn't hear his voice at first because I was minding my own business, but I slowly became aware that someone was singing along with me. When I looked up, Stefon was standing next to me, singing the song. I stopped singing and pulled my headphones off, but he kept going. His voice and pitch were on point, and he had a really strong sound. I was instantly impressed and started singing with him. We harmonized perfectly right from the beginning. I hadn't had that much fun since my group in college. He was able to do runs and hit every note right in time with the music. The song continued to build, and we got louder and louder, just feeding off one another's energy. The bus came to a sudden stop, and we both almost fell over the seat. The bus driver stood up and told us to shut up or get off the bus. We laughed, sat back in our seats, and exchanged numbers so we could find each other later on.

Stefon was already in another group, but he invited me to one of their rehearsals and they asked if I wanted to join them. I told them I would, but I wanted to be the lead. They already had a lead singer, but they knew I was better than him. We came to an uneasy compromise with me taking the lead on new songs and him keeping the lead on songs they already knew. Any decent group will tell you there can only be one true lead; otherwise, the group will eventually have an issue and self-destruct. It didn't take long before a couple of guys in the group started challenging me. They didn't trust me and were tired of me constantly showing off to get attention. Looking back, I was probably in the wrong, but I didn't realize that at the time. The group decided to break up. One of the other members went with me while Stefon and the other lead stayed together.

Being in a duet was fine, but I knew we needed at least one other guy, if not two, to have a shot at a record deal. Jodeci, a quartet of two sets of brothers, was still hot and rising up the charts. I knew we had a better sound, if we could only add a couple of other guys with similar talents.

Enter JD, a member of the Gangster Disciples who was working with a management company in Chicago. The company had heard about me through the previous groups I had been part of. They arranged a meeting for the two of us. I wouldn't have thought that a Blackstone and a GD could work together, but the moment we heard each other sing, we knew we had to put aside our differences in the streets and form a group. His voice was incredible and blended perfectly with mine.

We got a new manager who liked our voices but wasn't the biggest fan of the guy I had recruited from Stefon's group. He convinced JD and me to kick him out and look for a different third. I felt bad for the guy because I had been the one who'd broken up his original group and now I was kicking him out of the group he'd helped me form.

Our new manager was lining up some shows for us while JD and I continued to look for a third, and possibly a fourth, for our group. We auditioned a couple different guys, but none of them had the right sound or the look we were going for. We were able to do a couple of shows, and the crowds were into us, but we knew we could do better if we had a fuller sound. I wasn't willing to settle. I knew we could be huge if we found the right guy.

A couple of months went by with JD and I performing as a duet. It was pretty clear that he wanted to take the lead, and that led to some infighting between us. I knew I had a voice as strong or stronger than JD's, but I also didn't want to break up our group because he was incredible. I had raw talent, but JD had actually listened to his teachers and was formally trained. We fought a lot, but it never got physical. Our voices always ended up bringing us back together. We knew we were great and that we'd always have each other's backs. We just had to find that third.

The shows continued, as well as the fights, but we found our groove. Between working, practicing, and a full slate of performances, we stopped actively looking for another member. Guys would occasionally approach us after a show and ask if we were looking for a third. By this time, JD and I knew what we were looking for and could tell within a few minutes whether a dude had it or not. They usually didn't, and we weren't about to compromise.

We continued to get bigger shows and different parties as our reputation grew. During one of the larger party shows, a guy named Axe came up to us and introduced himself. He had heard of us and had come to the show that night to see us live. He wanted to find out whether we lived up to the hype. Our sound impressed him, but he was already in another group. We talked some more and found out that he was a producer. JD asked if we could hear him sing. He was good, but he wasn't great.

The night went on and we agreed to keep in touch. JD called me the next day and told me he wanted to try getting Axe into our group. I told him he wasn't that good of a singer, so why should we compromise our sound for this guy?

"Fool, did you not hear me? He's a producer. We don't need him to be a phenomenal singer. We both know that you and I will be the leads. He'll just sing in the background, hit the ugly notes, and round out the sound. He can hold a pitch, and he's got the right look. Besides, we can sing, and he'll do the producing afterward. This makes us a legitimate group. Let's add him."

It made sense to me. We called Axe and told him we wanted him in our group and that we wanted him to start practicing with us the next day. He was so blown away by how much we wanted him that he quit his other group and joined ours. That's how Laid Baq was formed.

The three of us became as close as brothers. JD and I continued to fight and argue over things like who would be taking the lead, what song we should focus on, and where we should eat. Axe always seemed to be cool and collected. He'd watch the fights and laugh at us. We could always count on him to defuse a situation if it was starting to escalate too much. All of us knew we could harass each other the same way most families do and still have each other's backs if someone else were to start anything.

Even though the relationship was good between JD and me, I always wanted it to be better. I wished we had a true brotherhood like what he had growing up with his siblings. There was a piece of me that wondered what it would have been like if we had been actual brothers or at least grown up on the same street. We loved each other, and that translated to a level of loyalty I had rarely felt in my life. The proof of that brotherly love happened on more than one occasion, but there is one moment that always comes to mind when I think about the early days of the formation of Laid Baq.

Through the group's gig and my off-and-on jobs, I had managed to save enough money to finally move out of my mom's house. The Two Flat I found in the general neighborhood I grew up in wasn't much, but it was mine and it provided a place for me to practice with the group, relax, and host house parties. These parties were usually on the weekend, and it was a normal occurrence for people I didn't know to show up. I didn't really care as long as people were having a good time and no one was starting any trouble, especially with my people. That's why I didn't pay any attention when a strange guy randomly showed up at my house during one weekend.

He came later in the evening. The music was good and the drinks were flowing. I was having a great time dancing with some girls I didn't know when I heard someone shout, "Gun!" right behind me. I turned and saw JD pointing a gun at the guy about two feet from me.

"Get away from him, nigga," JD said.

A couple of people screamed in terror, and there was a mad rush for the door as the house quickly cleared. No one liked being at a party where a gun was pulled, even on the South Side. The guy looked a little shaken, but I could definitely tell he was also pissed. Before I could say anything, JD yelled again.

"Get the fuck out of here, and don't ever come back."

The guy looked at me, then back at JD, and left.

Axe had appeared behind JD by this point. The house was empty except for the three of us.

"What the hell was that all about?" Axe asked before I could.

JD put the gun away and tried to explain. "I don't know who that guy was or why he was following Will, but I noticed him as soon as he walked in. He just seemed kind of off."

Axe interrupted. "Yeah, I noticed that too. He was kind of staring at Will and staying off to the side. I didn't pay him any attention."

"You should have," said JD. "He started off on the sides but continued to work his way closer to Will. I was planning on just saying something to him until I saw the knife on his belt."

"Woah," I said. "Woah, woah, woah! He had a fucking knife?"

"Yeah, I think he was really going to try and fuck you up, Will. That's why I pulled the gun on him," JD said.

The fact that JD pulled a gun didn't really surprise me that much. He'd had that gun on him almost always since I'd first met him. He loved that thing, and he felt it kept him safe. It was the one part of the streets he was not going to give up. What surprised me was that JD was ready to waste this guy and likely go to prison for a long time to protect me. At that moment, I knew that no matter what we were fighting about or what might happen in the future, JD and I would always be brothers.

The three of us got into the routine of songwriting, practicing, and producing. We wrote some original songs and started getting booked to bigger venues. JD and I continued to fight, but we had passion and wanted to see how far we could take our group. A guy named Cologne signed on to manage us. He was the radio station manager at WGCI, and it made sense for us to have someone who could really promote us.

Cologne came through almost immediately. He was talking with Steve Harvey from The Steve Harvey Morning Show. We had a spotlight coming up at a place called The Click that Cologne was helping us promote. Steve asked Cologne about our unknown group, and Cologne came right out and said we sounded better than Jodeci! Harvey, sounding almost offended, responded with, "Ain't no one better than Jodeci. You sure, man?" Cologne put it all on the line and said, "I'm sure. Come and see them."

As though this weren't enough pressure, we found out that Mary J. Blige, Dr. Dre, and a few producers from Def Jam had heard about the spotlight through the station and Cologne. Mary J. happened to be looking for some backup singers and a new group with a fresh sound she could work with. We got word that she would be at our show, in the front row. JD, Axe, and I knew that if we pulled this off, it would be the break we were looking for. Who knew what might come out of it? Record deals, tours, fame. It was all on the line.

For a moment, I flashed back to the last time I had felt this kind of pressure. The college show where my voice had cracked. I remembered that humiliation and how I had walked off the stage with my confidence shattered, and doubt began to creep into the corners of my mind. Could I really do this? Would my voice crack again? Would I let everyone down? But another voice crept in and began to scream loudly—a voice I wasn't used to listening to. It sounded like seven-year-old Will, dancing around and singing in his Spider-Man pajamas to Michael Jackson, full of confidence and loving music for nothing more than the sake of the music. I knew this voice, and I knew this kid. I knew what needed to be done at The Click, and I knew I could do it. I was going to sing my ass off and see which doors opened next.

The Click was packed that night, and we could feel the mix of expectation and tension in the air. There wasn't an empty seat in the house. The waitstaff loved these kinds of nights because they knew as long as the performance was good, people would have a good time, and the tips would be huge. The intro act took the stage and got everyone warmed up. Drinks were already being served, and the vibe was relaxed. We ran through our own warm-up, and the stage manager gave us the one-minute warning.

That minute might have been the longest of my life aside from the time I had that gun pointed at my head. The rush of nerves and anxiety was almost too much to bear. My stomach churned and my mouth went dry. The old self-doubt returned, and for a brief moment, I thought I might puke. JD had a similarly ill expression on his face, but before I could ask him if he was okay, the crowd erupted into applause as the intro act finished their last song and we were announced. The stage manager slapped us on the back and wished us luck.

The lights went out, and we took our spots in front of the mics. Somewhere in the silent darkness, a person coughed. I took a breath and smelled the cigarette smoke still hanging in the air. This was it. The music started, and the lights slowly came up. We dove into our first song, and within the first few notes, someone screamed, then another, and I was transported back to the college talent show with all those ecstatic girls. I glanced over at JD, and he was looking at me. We both grinned and winked at each other. We knew what was about to happen.

At first, Mary J. didn't show much emotion. She clapped and snapped her fingers, but I couldn't get a good read on her. I knew she could see everything happening around her—the crowd and the energy—but she seemed to tune it all out and care only about what we were doing on stage. I caught her staring at me and noticed she was following my moves and voice. This was my opportunity. I tuned everything else out and stared back like she was the only person in the room. My voice never sounded so good, and the longer I held her gaze, the more engrossed she became. It seemed like she'd stopped breathing or was at least holding her breath. Her mouth hung open in amazement, and there was an emotion in her eyes that I still can't describe. I think if it had been just the two of us, she would have eaten me up, right on that stage.

There are certain moments in life when everything comes together. The hard work, the environment, the opportunity, and even a little luck all seem to be on your side. Those moments when everything goes right. This was one of those defining moments. The world and everything in it disappeared for the brief hour we were on stage and nothing mattered but the next note. The crowd and waitstaff were so into it that no one worked for that hour. Everyone simply watched us sing, and no one complained about their empty glasses because they were so into our performance. The wait staff confirmed they had never seen the club come to a standstill like that before. The show ended, and the place erupted with applause and shouts of approval. We received a standing ovation from everyone in the club! JD, Axe, and I hugged each other and jumped up and down backstage. We were shrieking like high school girls and high-fiving each other.

"Did you see the way Mary J. Blige was looking at me?" I asked.

"Damn, Will. She wanted you right then and there!" Axe replied.

I laughed at him. "Well, hopefully we made a good impression."

"You sure did," said an unknown but slightly familiar female voice from behind us. We all turned, and there she was. None of us said anything. We were all kind of star-struck. Mary J. smiled, probably used to this kind of reaction.

"You guys have a great sound. I'm glad I came in tonight. When does your record come out?" she asked.

"Record?" JD said. "We ain't got no record. We don't have a label."

"Really?" Mary J. said, sounding surprised. "Well, in that case, give me your number. I want to help you get a deal. We're gonna make you guys huge."

Axe gave her his number, and she thanked us and said her manager would give us a call.

As soon as she was gone, we started shrieking again.

That night in the VIP room, we partied harder than ever before. Over liters of liquor, we relived the performance and the conversation with a pop icon. Any new person who entered the room got the full story in exhaustive detail. In our minds, we were big time, and this was just the beginning of the life we had been dreaming about for years. Nothing. Nothing could bring us down.

chapter 12

I woke up with a hangover from hell the next morning and didn't feel normal until the following day. JD and I kept calling Axe, asking if he had heard anything from Mary J.'s manager. He kept telling us to be patient, that the manager would call—just give it time. At the same time, our relationship with Cologne had come to an abrupt end.

After the show at the The Click, we had decided to try signing on with Lyor Cohen at Def Jam. He had been at the show, too, and we knew he could take us further in the business than Cologne ever could. We tried a few different angles to get him on the phone and talk about working with us, but nothing seemed to move forward. In a last-ditch effort, we called his office and left a message letting him know we were interested in him repping our group.

A couple days later, I got a call from Cologne.

"Yo, what you niggas *doing*?" he yelled over the phone.

I didn't know what to say and was kind of shocked by his sudden call.

"I got a call from Lyor over at Def Jam. Tells me you're trying to get him to sign on and manage you guys. Wants to know what's going on and why I'm not calling him."

We were found out, and I couldn't deny it. There was nothing I could say, so I just let Cologne keep tearing into me.

"After the show at The Click and all the shows I've lined up for you, everything I've done for you three, this is how you repay me. I'm done." And he hung up the phone.

I called JD and Axe and told them what had happened.

"Well, I guess we gotta find a new manager," JD said.

It didn't take long for us to find representation, especially with the offer from Mary J. still hanging out there. She had told us she would call, and we trusted she would. We just didn't know when.

A couple of days turned into a couple of weeks. Then a couple weeks turned into a couple of months, and we still hadn't heard anything. Maybe this wasn't our big break after all. We kept practicing and waiting, hoping we'd hear something. After six months, I was starting to lose hope. We were still getting three to four shows a week. Labels and managers also continued to call, and we continued to turn them down, waiting for the call from Mary J. She had told us she wanted to work with us, so we held on to that belief.

The music business for a group act is even more cutthroat than for solo artists. The show at The Click had put us on the map, and we were on everyone's radar. Managers, producers, and executives all knew we had a sound they could sell, but they also knew we were committed to working with Mary J. Blige. She was the only person who had spoken to us directly and wasn't playing the "my people will call your people" game. We respected that, and we believed in her. We continued to get calls from other labels and managers wanting to talk about a deal, but we turned them all down.

Our live performances continued around Chicago, and we started to get shows outside the city, as well. Over the summer, we got a call to go and perform at a showcase in Atlanta. We decided it would be good publicity and would keep our names relevant while we continued to wait on the call, so we went.

The show was a pretty standard lineup of new and upcoming artists. We were one of the final acts and were considered to be a real feature for the crowd. The show went off without a hitch, and the audience loved us as much as they had in Chicago. JD and I were talking offstage after our performance when the guy running sound approached us.

"Hey, guys. Great show!" he said with a smile.

"Thanks, brother," JD said. "Nice work on the soundboard. You're really talented."

"Thanks," he replied. There was an awkward silence. I could tell the sound guy wanted to say something else, but he was trying to figure out how to start. He finally took a breath and just went for it.

"Just so you guys know, one of the other managers came up to me after you guys had warmed up and just before you were going to take the stage. He offered me a good amount of cash to mess up your audio and make you look bad. I thought about it for it a second and probably would have done it if it were another group. But you guys are from Chicago. I'm from Chicago. We don't mess around with our own, so I told him to fuck off."

Having cleared his conscience, he told us he loved our act and wished us well in the future. I never saw that guy again, but stuff like that—sabotage—continued to happen.

The music business is brutal. It seemed like at least once a week, one of us would get a call from a different manager or producer asking us to either sign with them or split off from the group and start a solo career, but we were loyal, maybe to a fault. We had all but given up after waiting more than eight months for Mary J. to call Axe back. There was no way she still had his number, even if she did want to get in touch with him. She had probably forgotten about us anyway. Then, JD and I got a call from Axe.

"You guys, I think I just hung up on Mary J. Blige," he said.

"What you talking about, fool?" JD asked.

"This lady called, told me she was Mary J. and that she was ready to work with us. I hung up because she told us that night at The Click that her manager would be the one to call me. Why would she call me direct?"

JD was about to lose his mind.

"Call her back!" he screamed.

"I don't have her number, man. That's why I'm calling you guys. Do you have it?"

"We don't have her number, fool! You were the only one who got her info."

"Oh, yeah," Axe said. And he hung up.

JD and I just looked at each other.

"What the fuck just happened?" he asked. "Of all of us to get a number from, she gets his!"

We sat in silence for what seemed like an eternity, both afraid that if we talked, we might miss Axe's call. We both jumped when the phone finally rang.

Axe was talking so fast and so frenzied that we could barely understand him.

"Slow down, man. Slow down. What's going on?" JD said.

Axe paused, took a breath and said, "Mary J. called me back after we got off the phone. She told me it was really her and to stop playing. She sounded kind of pissed. I apologized and told her it wouldn't happen again. Guys, she wants to sign us to a contract!"

There was a brief pause as we all registered what Axe had just said.

"Guys, you still there?" Axe asked.

"You're not playing, right? This is real?" JD said.

"Yeah man, this is real."

JD and I looked at each other and jumped up, screaming in celebration. He dropped the phone, and we hugged each other and started jumping up and down, yelling our heads off. Neither of us said any real words until we finally calmed down a little and heard Axe's voice shouting from the phone on the floor.

"Guys, guys! Hey, you okay? What's going on over there?"

JD picked up the phone. "Get your ass over here, Axe. It's time to celebrate!" And he hung up.

Axe showed up to party and give us the details. It had taken so long to hear back because Mary J. had been busy putting her label together. She wanted to bring us on as one of her premiere acts alongside a couple of other groups. We were going to New York in a few days to do some recording. She had lined up the airline tickets, hotels, and transportation. All we had to do was show up, cut a track with her producer in the morning, and then record with her that afternoon. She wanted to get our group recorded and establish our sound with her first, then we would work on the songs we had written and put together our first album.

I didn't sleep much the next two nights; we practiced our set to make sure we were ready to go with whatever they threw at us. We met at the airport and boarded our flight, excited for the opportunity that lay ahead in New York City. Mary J. told Axe that her driver would pick us up at JFK and to look for our group's name on a board at the Arrivals gate. Sure enough, as we exited the airport, there was a guy all dressed up in a suit and cap. I couldn't wait to get into our limo and go to the studio. The driver walked us to a Lincoln Towncar. I almost asked him what was going on, where was the limo, but thought better of it and climbed into the back with JD, Axe, and our business manager.

We had our instructions—unload at the hotel and go to the first studio, record a track that Mary's producer had ready for us, then head over to Mary's studio to back her up that afternoon—but as we drove into the city, JD and Axe got a different idea.

"Let's show that producer what we can do," JD said. "We have so much of our own music, and we can really sing it. Maybe if we impress him enough, we'll have the record deal done before we leave the city tomorrow."

Axe agreed, but I wasn't so sure. "Come on, man. Why don't we just do what Mary J. told us?" I asked.

"Who knows if we'll get an opportunity like this again?" JD replied. "What's it hurt to sing a couple of our songs and see if he likes them?"

I wasn't convinced but figured we didn't have anything to lose. We all agreed we'd do a couple of songs and then record what Mary J. had laid out for us. There should be plenty of time, and it couldn't hurt.

We dropped our stuff at the hotel and the Towncar took us to the production studio where we were supposed to record the first track. By that time, I had been in many other recording studios, and there was nothing special about this one. It was a typical studio layout. There was a small room with a full soundboard that the production staff sat in and a larger recording room separated by a Plexiglas wall. This allowed the staff to see us and communicate with us while also keeping any noises they made from leaking onto our recording.

We sat in the lobby while the producer finished whatever he was working on and discussed our plan to sing some of our songs. JD began the conversation while Axe and I backed him up. Mary J. had told us that we would have a couple of hours in this studio before heading to hers. It wouldn't take us that long to record the song she wanted. As long as we got that done, did it matter what we did with the rest of the time we had?

The producer called us in, and we got behind our mics. He played the track we were supposed to sing and let us run through it a little. Then JD suggested we sing some of our original music. It was pretty clear that the producer wasn't interested, but he was also getting paid and didn't really care what we recorded as long as he got his cash. He told us to knock ourselves out.

We ran through almost an entire show set in less time than it should have taken. No warm-ups, no vocal breaks, not even that much water between songs. We were so new to this we wanted to impress anyone we could. If we only impressed the right people, they would help us along with Mary J. and the rest of our music career. Our stuff was good. We just needed the right person to hear it and figured this producer might just be that person.

The problem was, he wasn't. He wasn't the right person and we weren't in the right opportunity. Mary J. had given us and the producer specific instructions to record one track. She wanted it as a demo so she could use it to help us land a full record deal. Our naivety and inexperience also wasted my voice because I still hadn't fully learned how to use my diaphragm. Without the vocal breaks, I ended up completely losing it before we were able to finish recording the original track Mary J. had requested. Our time was up, and all we got recorded was the hook of the song. My voice was gone, and we had to go to Mary's studio with only a half-finished song. On top of it, the producer hadn't seemed impressed with us at all. The plan was a failure.

We were all pretty quiet on the short ride from the first studio to Mary's. JD went to use the bathroom while Axe and I waited in the lobby for her to arrive. The difference between her studio and the one we had just been at was crazy. The sound board was massive—at least twice the size of the previous one—and the recording room was huge and had a full drum set, a keyboard, and other instruments for whatever the track might need. This was big-time.

Axe was getting nervous. He knew my voice was shot and didn't know what we were going to do. I tried to calm him down and keep him from freaking out, but I was worried about it too. The only thing I could do was drink some water and hope at least a decent sound would return.

I was telling Axe it was all going to be fine when we heard some shouting from down the hall. "He did *what?*" said an angry female voice. "That motherfucker. Who does he think he is?"

Right then, we both realized the voice was Mary J.'s. Axe and I looked at each other. "Damn," Axe said. "Who do you think she's talking about?"

"Don't know, but I'm glad it's not me," I respond. Axe agreed. We sat in silence as the rant continued for minutes. It was so crazy, we didn't even notice JD come back and sit down with us. Eventually, the yelling stopped and Mary went into her studio. She came out a second later and motioned for us to come in.

"Where's the rest of it?" she asked, still upset and annoyed.

We looked at each other, confused. One of us managed to ask, "The rest of what?"

"The rest of the song you were supposed to record. You were over there for over two hours working. I gave you a song, and this is only the hook. Why you playing? Where's the rest?"

It dawned on me that we had messed up—again. All three of us spoke at the same time, trying to explain what had happened and why there wasn't a full song on the tape she was holding. The more we talked, the more annoyed and angry she got.

"Forget about it," she finally said. "Just get in the studio, and let's record the backup vocals."

They ran the song for us, and I knew our opportunity with Mary

J. and the contract she had offered was over before the song had finished. The song itself was a female-driven track with female backups
and lyrics. It made no sense for us to be on it. I also sounded awful,
my voice still gone no matter how much I tried to will it back. The
people on the other side of the Plexiglas had looks of pity more than
anything else. The session ended early, and we grabbed our stuff to
head back to the hotel.

None of us said anything as we headed to the elevators. We were
all too defeated and upset with ourselves. It didn't make sense for us
to talk. I realized about halfway there that I had left my water bottle
back at the studio. I told JD and Axe to go on, and I'd meet them at
the car. No one said anything when I came back looking for my bottle. I grabbed it and headed back to the elevators. The doors opened,
and I felt a tap on my shoulder. It was Mary J. and her sister.

"Mind if we ride with you?" she asked.

I managed to squeak out a "sure," and they got on.

No one spoke for a floor, then Mary J. turned to me and said,
"Your business manager almost got in a fight with one my boys, Will.
That was who I was yelling at up there."

I didn't say anything. What could I? We had wasted our recording opportunity from earlier in the day, we had lost our chance at the
biggest contract in our career, and now I'd found out that it was my
business manager who had caused her to be so upset earlier.

"Be careful of your business manager," she said.

I replied, "I'm loyal."

"Okay," was all she said back, but I could see in her eyes that
she was driving home the warning that my business manager was no
good and that this was the final opportunity I would have to work
with her if I made the wrong choice. We got off the elevator, and I
headed to the car.

The driver took us back to the original studio. I wasn't sure what was going to happen at this point; it seemed like we had completely blown our shot. The recording studio had a couple of extra people in it, and we were instructed to finish our original track with them providing additional vocals. Mary J. waited in the lobby for us to finish. We wrapped up, and I went to talk to her. She told me we'd hear from her, and she walked away. That was the last time I would ever see Mary J. Blige.

I told Axe and JD about our conversation in the elevator, but as I heard myself recalling the story, I got more and more upset. Later that night, I called our business manager for his perspective. He told me he'd almost gotten into a fight with one of Mary J.'s people because they were disrespecting him. I asked him how they'd disrespected him, and he couldn't answer the question. He kept repeating only that he'd been disrespected. Looking back, I wondered if he hadn't been paid by Cologne or someone else to sabotage us on that trip because he never did give me a straight answer or any real reason for starting that fight.

Over the next several days, I tried calling Mary J. I wanted a chance to explain what had happened, maybe to apologize and get a shot at redemption. One afternoon, she finally answered with an angry and annoyed, "*What?*" Her tone told me everything. It was over. There would be no second chance. I apologized for bothering her and hung up.

The next morning, I told JD and Axe that if we didn't fire our current business manager, I was done with the group. They tried to talk me down, but I'd made up my mind. It turns out my threat of leaving the group didn't matter because before the end of the year, I would be out anyway, but for completely different reasons.

chapter 13

I loved Chicago, but it didn't love me.

The thing most people will never understand is that no matter how much you try to get out of the streets and leave gang life behind, it always has a way of pulling you back in. I tried to escape it when I moved in with my dad, but I got pulled back in. I tried at Western Illinois University for two years, but I got pulled back in. Music seemed to be my real way out—it provided an ongoing relief—but when we got back from New York and our missed opportunity, I ended up right back where everything had started, the South Side. I got pulled back in.

I was pissed off and took out my frustration in unhealthy ways, which ended up getting me in trouble with the police, and I knew if I stayed in the hood, I'd either end up in jail or dead. I had to get out and leave Chicago for good. I needed to start over somewhere new where I could leave the thug mentality behind and not have to worry about it creeping back in. The only person I knew who lived far enough away was my brother Phil, who was still in Iowa. Des Moines would have to do.

Phil picked up his phone on the second ring, and I told him what was going on. I explained how I had to get out of Chicago and needed a place to lay low. I was getting into too much trouble there. He didn't hesitate.

"Pack up your stuff and drive to Des Moines. You can live with me for however long you need until you figure this out," he said.

I thanked him, hung up, started packing, and just like when I'd moved in with my dad in high school, all of my stuff fit into a single garbage bag. I said good-bye to my mom and headed west on Interstate 80, leaving Chicago in my rearview mirror.

The drive to Des Moines only takes about five hours. About ten miles west of Chicago, the city all but disappears behind you, and there is nothing but corn and soybean fields until the Iowa border. The interstate is straight without any hills or curves. What I'm trying to say is, it's boring. There are no distractions and nothing to hold your attention, so it gives anyone who drives it plenty of time to think.

My thoughts ran in a circle alongside the passing mile markers. What am I doing? What am I going to do with my life? How am I going to survive in a new place where I don't know anyone? Am I making a huge mistake? Will I be able to pull this off?

I thought more than once about pulling off the road and turning around. I was confused and unsure about what I was driving toward, but I knew it had to be better than what I was leaving behind. That thought kept me on the road and brought me to my brother's driveway. I sat in the car for a few more minutes, reminding myself that I was with family and everything was going to be okay. Eventually, I worked up the courage to grab the garbage bag from the backseat and head up to the door.

Phil greeted me with a hug and welcomed me into his home. He gave me a quick tour of the place and then led me to the room I would be staying in. His wife and three kids had followed us around for most of the tour. I could tell that his wife was anxious about having me in the house. She was tolerating me because I was Phil's kid brother, but it was clear she wouldn't hesitate to kick me out if I made any mistakes. Her distrust annoyed me because it felt like a piece of Chicago was following me. I was here to start over and build a new life. I didn't need her judgment when she didn't even know me yet.

As I was unpacking, Phil surprised me with a request for money.

"Will, I need $100. Any chance you have some spare cash you could give me?"

"Of course," I said, and pulled out my wallet.

"Thanks, man. And let's keep this between us, okay?" he said.

I nodded.

We had dinner and turned on the TV. Phil's wife was cleaning up the kitchen when she appeared in the doorway and asked Phil to come talk to her. She looked upset. They talked in whispers, and I could tell something was off, but it was my first night in their house and I wasn't about to interrupt. I had no idea what their relationship was like, and it wasn't up to me to interfere in whatever was going on.

Phil came back and sat down next to me. He didn't say anything, but I could tell he was annoyed. His wife finished cleaning the kitchen and went to bed without saying goodnight. I thought about saying something, but I figured it was best if I just minded my own business. We watched a couple more shows, and I told him I was ready to go to bed.

"Will," he said with a tension in his voice.

"Yeah?"

"Just so you know, my wife thought you had taken some money from the top of the fridge. That was what we were talking about in the kitchen."

I sat without saying anything, still trying to figure out what he

WILLPOWER   119

was talking about and why she thought I would steal from them. He continued.

"She said there was forty dollars on top of the fridge, and while she was cleaning, she could only find twenty. I told her she probably misplaced it or one of the kids took it. Told her it wouldn't make sense for you to take it.

I finally came to my senses. "You're right," I said. "If I was going to take the money, I would have taken the whole thing, not just half. That way, you would have thought you had misplaced it or that it was somewhere else. It doesn't make sense to just take half of it." I was getting pretty pissed now. I didn't like being accused of stealing from my brother, especially after I had just given him $100.

"Don't worry about it, Will. I'll take care of it," Phil said. He could tell I was getting hot. Thankfully, I didn't hear about the $20 again. I'm still not sure if one of the kids had taken it, if Phil himself had taken it, or if his wife had been mistaken about how much money had been there in the first place. It sure as hell wasn't how I wanted to start my life in Des Moines.

Their kids were great, though. They welcomed me with open arms, and it felt good to be a part of their lives. I was excited to have the opportunity to build a relationship with my niece and nephews. We'd wrestle and play games, but one of our favorite activities was singing and performing together. They had heard and seen recordings of me singing when I was in Laid Baq, and they loved it when I sang with or for them.

After the first week, I figured I should probably get a job and not just sit on my butt in my brother's house all day. Plus, it would give me the opportunity to show his wife that I wasn't a screw-up who couldn't be trusted. Phil was the manager at Garfield's Restaurant on the south side of Des Moines by Southridge Mall. It was a typical bar/restaurant that served burgers and domestic beer. He hired me as a dishwasher and told me that if I showed up on time and was good with the other staff, I would likely be able to move up to the cooking line in no time.

I kept my head down and washed dishes for the first couple of weeks. There was no issue with my attendance, and Phil was happy with what I was doing. No one mentioned my scars, and everything seemed to be going well. Like Popeye's, this wasn't my dream job, but it kept me busy and gave me some extra money to pay Phil for staying with him.

Like any restaurant with a bar, Garfield's had its regulars. Most of the people who showed up were looking for an escape or a drink before heading home, but there was one guy who always took it too far. He would show up either half-drunk already or would get completely hammered at the bar. If the bartender tried to stop serving him, he'd yell and try to start a fight. If we'd been in Chicago, he would have been kicked out and not allowed back in, but for some reason, in Des Moines, they kept letting him return no matter how much trouble he caused. He loved to berate the bartenders and hit on the waitresses even though he was already dating one of them.

One night, after drinking too much again, he pushed the shift manager and most of the staff past the breaking point. The manager burst through the kitchen door and shouted in frustration, "I wish someone would just do something about that asshole. He needs to get out of here."

I raised my head from the plate I was washing and said, "Shit, I'll do it." The manager looked at me with shock and relief on his face. My Chicago side was ready to come out and with the manager's permission, I wasn't worried about getting in trouble. He looked over at me and nodded.

The dude causing the trouble was running his mouth at the bar and was already pretty drunk. I walked up behind him and politely told him he had had too many drinks and needed to leave. He spun around on his barstool and looked me up and down, trying to decide whether he wanted to push the issue or not. After a brief pause, his liquid courage got the best of him.

"What'd you say, nigga?" he asked.

"Man, you gotta leave," I told him.

"You gonna make me?"

This was all I needed. I grabbed him around the waist and slammed him to the ground. The waitstaff and customers all stepped back, and I heard an audible gasp from a couple of people. He was on his stomach, and I was on top of him with his arms held back and my knee in the middle of his back.

"You gotta leave, bro," I said.

"Man, Imma sue all of you. Get off me! You can't put your hands on me," he yelled as he struggled to get free.

"You can sue whoever you want, but you gotta leave," I told him.

He tried to get free, and after a minute, he finally gave up. I helped him to his feet and escorted him out the front door.

"You're not welcome here anymore. Don't come back," I told him as he kept threatening a lawsuit. The waitstaff and manager thanked me for taking care of him, and I got back to my dishes. It felt good to have people scared of me again. I wanted respect and for people to know who they were messing with. This had given me that opportunity, and we never saw that guy in Garfield's again.

I kept to myself and did my job, and after a while, I was promoted to a position as a cook. The money was better, and I enjoyed it more than washing dishes for eight straight hours, but the restaurant scene wasn't where I wanted to be. The hours were long, and the pay wasn't enough to keep me interested in the next promotion. Plus, I really didn't enjoy Garfield's as a restaurant. Phil decided to look for new work, and shortly after he left, I did too.

Over the years, I'd gotten pretty jacked working out and was intimidating to look at, especially with my scars. The skinny kid from high school was long gone, and I enjoyed the fact that people were frightened when they looked at me. Phil had been a bouncer at a local club called City Lights while he was managing at Garfield's and suggested that I come bounce with him. It made sense to me. Bouncing gave me the chance to make some good money and occasionally work out my anger issues. I wasn't afraid to take a swing if necessary, but I still wanted to avoid fighting if at all possible.

Being a bouncer had its drawbacks, especially the constant disrespect from dudes wanting to impress their friends or girlfriends. But it also had its perks, mainly the attention I'd get from the ladies. There was no shortage of women who wanted to skip cover or sneak in when the club was already full. Most of the time, it wasn't worth the trouble, and I'd make them stay in line. Occasionally, I'd let one or two of them in.

One night, a girl showed up, and we started talking while she was in line. She was cute and told me she had just broken up with her boyfriend. It was pretty evident she was a couple of drinks in already and was out on a rebound night. I had these conversations all the time with girls in line and didn't think anything of it. She had her ID and wasn't too drunk, so I let her and her crew in.

An hour later, a group of guys showed up. The club wasn't very busy, and there wasn't anything unusual about them, so after checking their IDs, I let them in. A couple minutes after I had let this group of guys in the club, I got a call on my headset. Some punk in the club was pissed because his girlfriend was flirting with the front door bouncer. It turns out the ex-boyfriend had come to the club looking for his girlfriend and wanted to fight "the ugly bouncer out front with the scars on his face."

That comment sent me over the edge. I was ready to fight right then and there. I burst through the door and headed toward the center of the club where he was standing with his friends.

"You gonna fight me over some pussy?" I screamed in his face. "Jump me right here, right now!"

His boys looked at him, and he looked at me, not sure what to do.

"You wanna jump me over a girl? That's bullshit. Jump me right now!" I shouted again. He didn't move.

By this time, all the other bouncers had come up behind me. The call had been made over the headset to get inside and back me up. Phil came up on my right and stood between me and the other guy. The volume of the music had been lowered in case an announcement needed to be made to clear the place.

"If you're going to do something to him, you're going to do it to the both of us," Phil said.

"Man, we ain't got nothing with you," the guy replied.

"I know, but he's my brother, and this is my spot. You mess with him, you're messing with all of us."

The guy looked at my brother, then back at me and the rest of the bouncers. He glanced over his shoulder at his own crew—the friends who were supposed to be backing him up—but most of them had already taken a couple of steps back. He glared at me one more time and left the club, knowing he'd never win the fight with all of us. The music picked back up, and people started partying again like nothing had happened.

Phil looked at me. "Man, what's wrong with you?" he asked.

I was still high on the adrenaline, and his question caught me off-guard. "What you mean, what's wrong with me? That fool was starting shit, and I was going to finish it."

"Yeah, I know you would, Will. You're always ready to fight. Someone looks at you wrong, and you're ready to take their head off. I thought you were trying to get past that shit. That's why you moved here. We would have handled that guy. You didn't need to come in here and get in his face. You gotta learn to control the anger, bro."

The adrenaline was gone. Phil was right. What was wrong with me? Here I was, miles from Chicago and the streets, and I still wanted people to fear me. If they did, they respected me, and I wouldn't have to be afraid of them. At least that's what I kept telling myself. Did I really have to keep fighting people for them to respect me and fear me? And if I did, why had I left Chicago anyway?

City Lights had its regulars just like Garfield's. There were always guys looking to get laid and women looking for those guys. There were the normal drug dealers, occasional strippers, and people just looking to get away from the boredom of their average lives. Most people were just there to have a good time, and as long as they didn't get too out of control, we would let them.

One of the regulars was a girl we'll call Tasha, and she would come in with her friend Mindy. They were both cute, but I really wanted to get with Mindy. I tried several times, but she always turned me down. Tasha was always with her, and I figured I had blown my chance with her because I had hit on Mindy in front of her. They continued coming to the club, and Tasha and I started talking more, so I asked her for her number and she gave it to me.

Tasha was a good-looking girl with longer auburn hair and blond highlights. She had deep brown eyes, a great smile, and a nice body. Her face reminded me of Tracy Scoggins from Dynasty. For those too young to remember or even know who I am talking about, just Google her name. To me, she was fine.

We started talking on the phone regularly. I learned that she had a guy friend who was in jail and that she would go see him every now and then. I didn't want any part of that, and I told her that if she was going to be with a guy in jail, I didn't want to be around her. She told me she would stop seeing him, but I found out she'd lied to me.

I broke it off with her.

I'd already been dating another girl named Pam when Tasha and I'd first gotten together. Looking back, I realize that I was a hypocrite. I didn't want Tasha seeing anyone else, but it was fine in my head to date two women at the same time. At least by breaking up with Tasha, I was back to only seeing one woman. Pam was cute, and I had a good time when I was with her, but I couldn't get Tasha out of my head. There was another problem. Pam lived with her parents, and I was still at my brother's house, so it was difficult to find time alone. I knew early on that Pam and I would never work out long-term, but she was fun in the moment, so I kept seeing her.

Some time went by, and Tasha started calling again. I ignored her calls or sent her to voicemail. After all, I was dating Pam. A couple of days went by, and the calls stopped. I figured she had moved on or was back with the prison guy. Then a random number came up, and I answered. It was one of Tasha's friends calling to tell me that she'd finally broken up with her con and wanted to be with me. She asked me to take Tasha's call so she could explain. I agreed that the next time she called, I would pick up.

As soon as I hung up, Tasha called. She confirmed her friend's story—that she was done with the other guy and that I was the only guy for her—so I told her I'd give her another chance, but that I was done if I found out she was seeing anyone else. She agreed, and we started dating even though I was still seeing Pam.

Things continued to go sideways with my sister-in-law. She never trusted me, and I think she still thought I'd stolen that $20 when I'd first moved in. Worse still, she didn't think I was a good influence on her kids. I tried many times to prove that my past in Chicago hadn't followed me to Des Moines, but it didn't matter. My brother never said it, but it was pretty clear that I should start looking for my own place.

The need to search for a new apartment gained steam when my brother got a new job out of town and had to move. His wife and kids stayed in Des Moines because the new gig wasn't supposed to be long-term or permanent. Without Phil there, the tension between me and his wife escalated. I had to get out. Pam was still living with her parents, so I knew I couldn't move in with her. Tasha had her own place and was more than happy to have me move in with her. That made my decision pretty easy. I broke up with Pam and moved in with Tasha.

In the beginning, I think Tasha truly did have feelings for me. She made it clear right away that she was going to take care of all of the bills. By this time, she had been on her own for so long she didn't need the help. She enjoyed her independence and wanted to show me that she could handle life. I didn't need to come in and save her from anything.

Tasha worked at a club that had a massage spot in it called The Water Palace. She was up front with me right away and told me that she danced and gave massages in the nude. It was an attraction for guys with money who couldn't get a girl or dudes who were lonely and wanted an attractive woman to touch them. We talked about it, and she assured me that all she was doing was massaging them. The money was good, and I figured it didn't hurt that some perverts were willing to pay to see my girlfriend naked as long as that was all they were paying for. Besides, she always came home to me at the end of her shifts. We got along pretty well at first. There was the occasional fight, and I quickly realized she had some issues we were going to need to work through if this was going work.

It didn't take long for me to fall in love with her. Being around her all the time, sharing the house with her, and having great sex, I wanted to be with her, and I wanted her to be with me. Her schedule was always up in the air with the club and her other side gigs, but I always had a general idea of when she would be home or where she was each night. A couple of months into living with her, that started to change. She stopped coming home at the end of her shifts at the club, or she'd be a couple of hours later than normal. I started to ask questions, and we started to fight more regularly.

Her shifts at The Water Palace picked up, and so did the money coming in. She started coming home more infrequently. We started fighting about her schedule and the amount of time she was spending at work. She began using weed regularly, and our communication started getting worse. She couldn't explain where the extra money was coming from or why she continued to run later and later. In the back of my mind, I already knew why, but I wanted to hear it from her. Finally, she came home late after a shift at the club, and I met her at the door. I wanted to know what was going on, and we got into a huge fight. She finally confessed that she wasn't just massaging the guys. She was also a "working girl."

My heart broke, not just for me, but for her as well. I was deeply in love with her, and I couldn't believe this was the life she had chosen for herself. I knew I should leave, but I couldn't. She had this hold on me. We started fighting more. I became more paranoid about where she was going and who she was seeing. Every time she left the house, I'd interrogate her. Sometimes she'd answer, sometimes she wouldn't. A couple of times, her answers made me so mad and so disgusted that I wanted to hit her. I never did, but I came close.

Tasha shared a lot more with me after she confessed to having sex with other men. Most of the time, it was in the form of an argument or a fight. I learned she had been beaten up by an ex-boyfriend and molested, like me, by her stepfather. At one point, she had been homeless and lived on the streets. Her life hadn't been easy, and she had been through a lot in a short amount of time. She grew more attached to the black community than the white because she felt accepted there. She had a chip on her shoulder and wasn't afraid to fight if she needed to. I truly believed she was a good person, but she felt like she had to do what she was doing to survive. It wasn't that she wanted to be a working girl; she had to be.

Tasha's situation reminded me a lot of the decisions I had made growing up in Chicago. I had joined the Blackstones for safety and protection. I'd moved in with my father in order to survive. I'd left Chicago for Des Moines because it was the only way to keep myself out of trouble and to stay alive. I related more to Tasha than anyone else I had ever met. She wasn't good for me, and our relationship wasn't good for either of us, but I didn't care. I knew what she was going through, and I felt I could help her through it.

There's a difference between supporting someone you love and enabling them. At the time, I thought I was doing everything in my power to support Tasha and be a good boyfriend. It didn't occur to me until much later that the actions I was taking and the support I was providing were allowing her to continue along her downward spiral.

I continued to overlook the illicit sex and our fighting because I wanted to help her. She could have a different life if only she could make different choices. She just needed someone to show her.

My bouncing role continued at City Lights, but I also ended up getting a steadier job at Aaron's Rental Center. Aaron's was one of those rent-to-own places where you could buy a TV and pay retail or, if you didn't have the cash to buy it outright, put it on a payment plan. The hours were steady and allowed me to work during the day while I bounced at night.

Tasha was typically asleep during the day while I was at Aaron's, so it surprised me when she came into the store one afternoon. She had just gotten her hair done, and I was excited to see her because she never visited me at work. She had a look of concern and anxiety on her face. After a quick hug, I asked her what was up. She didn't pause or even take a breath to steady herself.

"I'm pregnant, Will."

I stood there for a second, not sure I'd heard her correctly.

"What?" I asked, kind of shaken.

"Will, I'm pregnant," she said, this time with a slight smile on her face.

My mind started to race. The doctors told me before I'd left the hospital that I was likely sterile. The various surgeries and radiation treatments I had received following the Gangster Disciples' beating had taken their toll on my body. I didn't care much about it when I was younger—in fact, it gave me more freedom to have sex because there was one less consequence I had to worry about—but the older I got, the more I realized how much I wanted a family, and it weighed on me that I wouldn't be able to have kids naturally.

I'm not sure how long I stood there not saying anything while I considered how my life was about to change, but it suddenly dawned on me that she was waiting for me to say something. I smiled and picked her up to hug her. She let out a deep sigh of relief as I set her back down. A thousand questions and thoughts tumbled through my mind, and after another pause, I said the only thing that mattered.

"I'm going to be a daddy."

She smiled. "Yes you are, Will," she said, and we kissed.

chapter 14

People ask me all the time, when did you turn your life around? What moment was it that made you realize you needed to make a change and do something else? The answer is always the same, and it's pretty simple—it was the day I knew I was going to be a father.

The day Tasha told me she was pregnant, everything changed. For the first time in my life, I had someone who needed me. When we found out we were having a little girl, it got even more real. My life was no longer just mine. It belonged to this child, and I was going to be the best dad I could be. I wanted her to look up to me as her hero. The part of me that had taken center stage in my life since I'd been molested, the monster that always wanted more attention, was silenced that day. I no longer needed the attention or the validation. All I needed was to support and love my baby girl.

Tasha and I had a serious conversation about her lifestyle and what she was doing to her body. I told her all the booze, weed, and sleeping around needed to stop. It wasn't good for her, and it sure as hell wasn't good for our unborn child. We didn't need to put the baby through all of that before she was even born, and I didn't want my daughter brought into this world with her mom using. Tasha resisted, but eventually agreed. The stripping and massage work stopped, and so did the sex. We were going to have a family.

I got a job at the post office and started bringing in some decent money for the first time in my life. The benefits were good, and it would mean that I could support Tasha and the baby. Tasha found some work and made some money too. It wasn't as good as what she was getting when she was stripping, but it was much healthier. Life was starting to come together, and I was really happy with the direction it was heading in.

Her due date was coming up, and we hadn't decided on a name. I told her I wanted to name the baby Sky. Growing up, I would watch *All My Children*, and there was a character named Skye Chandler. I don't remember anything about the character or even the actress who had played her, but the name stuck with me. When I found out I was going to have a baby girl, it was the only name I wanted. Tasha didn't feel the same.

"Sky? You want to name the baby Sky? Why?" I gave her my reasons, but she still had her doubts. "I don't want to name my first baby girl Sky," she said.

Tasha had already had two boys of her own with two other guys. While we were dating, I treated them like they were my own, but this was my first, and I wanted to name her.

"Tasha, you already got to name your two boys. You're gonna give me this one," I said. She finally relented, and Sky was born shortly after.

From the moment I laid my eyes on her, I knew she was mine. It didn't matter that her mom was a stripper and sleeping around with other guys. Sky was mine. I could feel it in my bones and in my heart. I loved that baby girl more than I'd ever loved anything. Even more than I loved myself. But people started asking if I was the father almost immediately.

"She looks like her momma, but I don't see you in there anywhere. You sure she's yours?" people would ask. Friends, family, and sometimes people I barely knew would throw this question out there like it didn't mean anything, like they were just talking about the weather or a movie they had just seen. They didn't think about what the question meant or the hurt it caused and the accusation behind it. It didn't matter though. Every time I was asked that terrible question, my answer was always the same. "Of course she is."

I wanted to give Sky the kind of childhood and life that I didn't have. The cycle of abuse and neglect was going to end with me. She was going to know what it was like to have a supportive and loving father. More than anything, I wanted to give her the love that I'd never received from my mom. I didn't want another person to go through a childhood like mine. Sky was going to know that her daddy loved her and that he'd do anything for her.

The post office job helped me put food on the table and provide for Tasha, her two boys, and Sky. It allowed me to support the people I loved, and I felt good about that. Shortly after Sky was born, Tasha asked me to marry her. I think she saw what I was trying to do and that I was a good man who could help her and her family. I turned her down, though, because even then, I knew in my heart that she wasn't marriage material. Sure, I was in love, more than ever. She'd given me my first kid, and no one else ever would, but she didn't respect me, and she was already starting to lie to me again.

Tasha loved to smoke weed, but I couldn't stand it. I tried many times to negotiate with her about the amount she was using. Other than during her pregnancy, I had never asked her to stop completely or give it up, just not to smoke too much.

"Give me three days, Tasha. Just don't smoke for three days,"

I pleaded one time. She agreed but made it less than two. Between the lying, the fights, and the drug use, things got so bad that we separated for the first time. I hated it. We had just had a kid together, my first kid, and now I couldn't see her when I wanted to. I couldn't be there when she needed me, and I couldn't be sure about what might be happening when I wasn't around.

We agreed that Tasha would have Sky during the week, and I would have her on the weekend. Each week, I counted down the days until Friday, when I would pick her up and hang out with her. I hated being away from my daughter, but I didn't want to be around Tasha if she was going to continue living her life the same way.

Shortly after we separated, I started seeing someone else. Tasha got pissed that I was seeing another girl and confronted me about it, so we started talking again. She asked me to move back in, told me she and her boys missed me, and that she needed me in her life. She insisted that she would change and start taking care of herself. No more weed and way less partying. She had taken a job at one of the larger corporations in town and was bringing in a steady paycheck, so I agreed in hopes that she would move on with her life. Living together again also made good financial sense. It was much cheaper.

Things did change for a while, but then she returned to old habits. She started smoking too much weed and hanging out with random guys again. I caught her lying to me about where she was going, whom she was with, and what they were doing. To make matters worse, she was incredibly violent when she got angry, a product of her upbringing and troubled past. She would lose her temper and shriek like she was possessed or try to start a fight with me. Many times, I had to physically push her off of me or restrain her in order to keep her from hurting one of us. But our first separation had pained me so much, I didn't want to go through it again. I was determined to try to make it work no matter what.

I should have left so many times, but I chose to overlook Tasha's faults and shortcomings. More than anything, I wanted Sky's mom and dad to be together. I so desperately wanted her to have the childhood and family that I didn't, but Tasha couldn't get over her past. I knew she loved me, but in the end, that love wasn't enough.

I realized she was never going to change. She still craved the street life. The club, the cannabis, other men continued to pull her away from me and her family. A piece of her wanted to change and be with me, but the rest of her couldn't imagine what I was trying to build or the life I wanted to lead with my new family. I was trying to make a better life and move on while she was stuck. There's no way to make something work when the only two people in charge are moving in opposite directions.

Our relationship finally ended when it got so heated that I almost lost my temper and physically assaulted her. I wanted to tear her apart. There were so many lies, and there was so much disrespect that I couldn't take it anymore. I knew that if I didn't leave, I might do something I would regret.

It was one of the hardest decisions of my life. Not only was I abandoning Tasha and Sky; I was also leaving her two boys. Off and on, Tasha and I had been together for almost six years. Her sons had grown attached to me, and they thought I was giving up on them. I couldn't make them understand that if it was in my power to work things out with their mom, I would have stayed. At one point, they asked if I had ever really loved them. In their eyes, someone who loved them wouldn't leave. They couldn't understand how leaving was an act of love.

Sky was three when I left Tasha for the last time. There aren't strong enough words to describe how terrible and lost I felt. In my eyes, I was a complete and total failure. Everything I had done had ended in disappointment. I'd dropped out of college, been fired from

Popeye's, lost a real shot at a music career because of ego, and now the one dream I wanted more than anything had exploded. I no longer had my family.

I turned to the only person I could. I called Phil. He and his wife had gotten divorced, and he was with a new woman. Moving back in with him wasn't my proudest moment, but he opened his home to me. My job at the post office continued to provide some decent funds; I gave Tasha any leftover money I had and was always there when Sky needed me. Even though I wasn't living with Tasha anymore, I still wanted to make sure she and Sky were supported and that my daughter knew her daddy loved her.

For months, my life was a blur. I was in a fog trying to understand what had happened and what I needed to do next. It seemed like no matter how hard I tried, life continued to beat me down. Every time I took a step forward into a new chapter, I'd fall down and have to start over at the beginning. I was tired, but I knew deep down I couldn't give up. That was the coward's way out, and I had never backed down from a challenge. I just needed to find a new opportunity. A couple of months later, on Thanksgiving Day, that opportunity found me.

chapter 15

Moving out of Tasha's house and leaving Sky behind left me in a dark place. The post office kept me busy on the night shift but didn't fill the time during the day. Phil's new girl didn't like me any more than his ex-wife had, and she'd made that clear pretty early on. She worked days, which meant she was usually gone by the time I got home from my shift. It worked well for both of us because it meant we didn't have to see each other often.

His girlfriend didn't want me using any of their stuff. I couldn't use their laundry detergent to wash my clothes, couldn't eat their food or drink their drinks. They had me paying $400 a month to have a tiny room in the basement, and I had to pay for everything else I consumed. There were times I caught his girlfriend getting into my stuff—the food and drinks I'd bought for myself to keep from using theirs—but that didn't matter to Phil. This was more her place than it would ever be mine, and I had to follow her rules.

At one point, I bought a giant bottle of laundry detergent and put it by the washing machine. It was so big, the kids had a hard time lifting the jug to pour detergent into the measuring cup without making a big mess. I told Phil's family that anyone could use it. I was done with the petty dividing up of everything, but it didn't make a difference. Phil wasn't going to stand up to her even if she was treating me like garbage. There was nowhere else I could go, so I dealt with it. I started to get into my own head and quickly realized that if I gave in to those ever-present negative thoughts, I'd be heading down an even darker path I didn't want to follow.

The winter holidays were fast approaching, which meant I had even more time to think about what I was missing with the family I had tried to create. The post office gave us Thanksgiving Day off, and Phil and his family did the normal holiday family thing. They let me eat with them, but I felt out of place the whole time. I wanted to get away for a few hours and chill.

Phil's place was close to a club called Razz Ma Tazz. It wasn't the best club in the city but it didn't need to be that night. All I needed was a place that provided me a chance to escape. I figured I'd go for a couple hours, have some drinks, maybe dance a little if some cute girls were there, and call it an early night.

As I walked through the front doors, it was a like a spotlight was on me. The place was pretty dark, and I'm not sure whether the lighting was meant to be that way, but it felt like something was about to happen, something big. There was a table with some girls and one guy at it. Other than a few other random people, the club was pretty empty. It was Thanksgiving Day, after all. I thought the girls at the table were attractive, so I walked by them on my way to the bathroom and took my jacket off as I passed by. I was wearing a sleeveless t-shirt underneath. Through the years of weight training and lifting, my arms had gotten pretty large, and these women noticed.

I took note that the table next to them was empty and decided to sit there when I came out of the bathroom. The girl on the end was the cutest, I thought, and I figured I didn't have anything to lose, so I tapped her on the shoulder.

"I'm sitting here all by myself on Thanksgiving. Would you mind coming over here to sit with me and chill for a little bit?"

She blushed and didn't say anything as she turned back to her friends. I heard mumbled whispers—"I think I know him," and "No you don't." I found out later that a couple of her friends had told her not to do it, to stay with them and avoid me, but she decided to come over anyway.

"What's your name?" I asked.

"Jai," she said. "What about you?"

"That's a pretty name. I'm Will," I told her.

It's funny how a single decision can shape a future. The decision to go to Razz Ma Tazz that night would have a lasting impact on me. All I was looking for was an escape from my life and to blow off some steam. Instead, I'd found Jai, and that's how our relationship started. A shoulder tap and an awkward introduction changed my life forever. And by the way, she wasn't supposed to be there either. Her friends had forced her to come out. Crazy, right?

We ended up talking for a while. I loved the flow of our conversation. It was easy to talk to her, almost effortless. We covered the basics—growing up, what we were doing now, why we were at the club on Thanksgiving. I learned that she had recently broken up with someone and was looking for a similar escape. Other than that, our conversation was pretty light, and I could tell she was into me too.

The music changed, and she started to move her shoulders a little. I took the opportunity to ask if she wanted to dance. She laughed and gave me a sideways glance, trying to figure out if I was serious or not, so I stood up and held out my hand. She took it, and as we headed to the dance floor I caught her looking back at her friends. A couple of them were dancing in their seats while a couple of others stared at us in disbelief.

The floor was pretty empty, and we started to move together, figuring out each other's style. It didn't take long to get into a rhythm. I pulled her in closer and told her she should rub my arms. Without hesitation, she put her hand on my left tricep and rubbed around to my bicep, then down on to my forearm. I had worked hard to build up the muscles, and I was proud of how they looked. Jai continued touching me, moving on to my right arm, and I could tell she really enjoyed them too. She smiled at me, and we continued dancing for a couple more songs, not really saying much.

A song neither of us knew came on, and we headed back to the table to continue our conversation. As we sat back down, a dude bumped into her and called her a "bitch." Jai could see me tense up. I was about to stand up and swing on him when she reached out and touched my hand.

"Don't worry about it, Will. It ain't worth it," she said.

"He can't just disrespect you for walking into you. It was his fault. He should be taught a lesson," I replied.

"That's sweet, but don't worry about it. Don't ruin a good evening because of that fool."

She talked me down, and we continued our conversation. Before either of us knew it, the club was closing. We exchanged numbers and went home. I called her as I got to Phil's place, and we continued talking the rest of evening until she left to go Black Friday shopping. I lay in bed after we hung up, and it struck me that I had just talked to one girl for an entire evening and most of the next morning and still wanted to keep talking to her. If she felt the same, then we must have something good going on.

We kept seeing each other, and I started to learn a little bit about her past—the guys she had dated, her baby daddy, and the things in life she was working toward. She told me she wasn't interested in anything serious because she was on her way out of a bad relationship that wasn't completely over yet. The guy she had been dating was still following her, stalking her, and she didn't want to bring someone new into her drama. I was so into her that I told her I didn't care. A part of me already wanted to protect her from whoever this guy was even though I had only just met her.

Three days later, I came down with a really bad case of the stomach flu. I couldn't keep anything down, and I was completely exhausted. Phil's family was nowhere to be seen, and the only person I wanted to see was Jai, so I called her.

She showed up a couple of hours later. I was lying in bed under a pile of blankets to fight the chills caused by the illness. My durag covered my head, so all you could see was my eyes, nose, and mouth. Jai came in and sat down beside me on the bed. She reached under the covers and held my hand. For a long time, we didn't say anything. We didn't need to. She sat there and rubbed my hand, smiling at me.

She came back the next day and the day after that. Like clockwork, she was there. She really wanted to be with me and care for me. As I started to feel better, we shared more stories and learned more about each other. It turned out that the guy she had just called it off with had wanted a deeper relationship with her than she was interested in. He was an alcoholic, too, and did a lot of drugs, but the stalking really messed with her. I wasn't too worried about it. This was nothing compared to what I had gone through in Chicago.

When I was feeling better, we started hanging out more, and Jai became more concerned with her ex's stalking. It was getting worse. He had figured out we were seeing each other, and while he didn't know who I was or what I looked like yet, he recognized the truck I was driving. I told Jai not to worry about it. I wasn't going to let anything happen to her, and I would take care of her ex if he ever tried anything with me. I didn't have to wait long.

A couple of nights later, we were having dinner at her place. We both heard a strange noise outside but didn't think anything of it. Her house wasn't in the best neighborhood, and strange noises were a regular occurrence. Another noise, this time closer, sounded like glass breaking. I rose from the table when a brick suddenly crashed through the front window.

"What the fuck?" I yelled as Jai let out a scream. We could see the street from the table. A guy was standing there with a brick in his hand, looking in through the broken glass.

"Shit!" Jai said with terror in her voice. "It's him!"

She didn't have to say anything else. I knew that this was her stalker and that he needed to be taught a lesson. He threw the brick and broke another window out while Jai let out another scream. I ran to the kitchen and grabbed the butcher knife from the silverware drawer, my blood boiling. I wasn't going to let anyone do this kind of thing to me, let alone someone I cared for. My memory of the streets came back in an instant. I was prepared to kill this guy if I needed to.

"Will, don't," Jai yelled and grabbed my wrist. Her touch caught me off-guard. For a brief moment, my rage subsided. No one had ever been able to take away my anger that way before. I looked into her eyes and saw the fear behind them. She wasn't worried about me getting hurt; she was worried about what would happen to me if I killed this guy. She was afraid to lose me.

I dropped the knife and held her hand for a split second. "I'll be fine," I told her and walked out the front door.

Her ex had picked up another brick and was about to throw it as I cleared the stairs. He looked at me, and his eyes grew wide. He wasn't expecting someone as big as me to come out of the house. I started running toward him, and he took a couple of steps back, but before he could turn and run, I was on him. My first swing hit him right in the jaw, and the second landed in his stomach. He doubled over and fell to the ground. I got on top of him and was about to punch him again when I heard sirens. Someone had called the cops.

It was then that I realized the original sound we had heard was him throwing bricks through my truck windows. They were all busted out along with the two windows in the house. Jai was standing in the doorway, staring at us. He started to struggle to get free, but I put him in a choke hold to keep him from going anywhere. The sirens got louder, and he started to struggle more, so I tightened my grip. At one point he told me to get off of him, told me I was choking him and was gonna kill him. I smiled and told him he should have thought about that before he'd thrown the bricks through our windows.

The cops rounded the corner and parked their cars in front of Jai's house. Jai's ex yelled out, "Help me! He's trying to kill me!" The cops rushed over and were about to arrest me when Jai ran out of the house to set things straight.

"No, you got it wrong. Arrest him. He tried to kill me. He threw bricks through the windows of the house and the truck. Will just helped me stop him and held him down until you got here."

They looked at her and looked down at the two of us. One of them tapped me on the shoulder and told me I could get off him. All I wanted to do was punch him one more time, but something in the back of my mind told me not to. Don't give them a reason to arrest you too. They picked him up, cuffed him, and led him to their car.

Jai burst into tears as I gave her a hug and told it would be okay. Her body shook under my embrace and I told her everything was fine. She reached up and touched my face and gave me a kiss, the salt from her tears running into our mouths. We stood on the front step for a while before going back into the house, holding each other.

We sat down at the dining room table, trying to figure out what to do about the broken windows when a knock at the front door caused Jai to jump and grab my hand.

"It's okay, Will. It's my dad. I called him after you went outside because I wasn't sure what was going to happen with you in the fight." She went to the door and let him in.

He joined us at the table as we made awkward introductions. Jai explained what had happened and how I had helped. He smiled at me.

"Well, this isn't exactly how I expected to meet you the first time," he said.

"Me, neither," I replied. We talked for a while, and when he could tell the situation had been defused and that we were okay, he went home for the night.

Jai and I sat at the table, talking about nothing important. I'm still not sure what had come over me in the moment. It could have been the adrenaline from the fight or the feelings I already had for Jai, but something told me that I needed to show her what I actually looked like. Up to this point, she had only seen me in a durag. My keloids had become really inflamed, and the ones on my ears were as big as golf balls. The rest of my head wasn't much better, but I felt like she needed to see it.

"Fuck it," I said out loud. Jai jumped a little at my sudden outburst. I realized I had been sitting in silence as all the thoughts about whether or not to uncover my scalp had raced through my head. "Look, I wasn't expecting this to be the way I showed you what I look like under this, but it needs to be done," I said, and removed the durag.

Up to this point, everyone I had ever met had gasped or stared awkwardly or turned away whenever they saw my keloids. The gazes of strangers on my deformed head, their frowns and hushed whispers, always made me feel like a monster. My appearance was something I had learned to be ashamed of and something I needed to hide. Especially when my keloids were inflamed like they were now.

I kept my eyes on the table, waiting for the normal gasp, but it never came. I looked up and caught Jai's eyes. She didn't look disappointed or disgusted. Her expression hadn't changed. She moved her hand to my face, slowly rubbing my chin and cheek, then gently touching the growth on my ear. She was supposed to be upset by my appearance, but instead, she simply smiled and said, "What's the big deal?" and gently kissed my forehead.

We talked for a couple of hours and boarded up the broken windows to keep her house warm. I told Jai I would stay the night. She was still in a bad spot, and I couldn't really blame her. As we lay in bed that night, she gently rubbed the keloids on my ears. We didn't talk much the remainder of the evening. She kept rubbing my ears and holding my hand. For the first time in a very long time, I felt normal. I felt loved, and I felt like someone saw me for who I truly was. She didn't have to tell me she thought I was handsome. Her actions did the work. Eventually, I fell into one of the most comfortable sleeps I have ever had.

chapter 16

It turns out that fighting Jai's ex and holding him down for the cops was the easy part of the ongoing situation between the two of them. We were told that Jai needed to press charges to start the process of getting a restraining order. It was also the only way for him to have any sort of consequences for his actions. If she didn't, he would simply walk away, and what kind of message would that send? She wanted to feel safe, and she wanted him out of her life. I agreed to help her in any way I could, but I was starting to have second thoughts about our relationship.

Jai was incredible, but did I really want this drama? The baggage she had with this ex-boyfriend wasn't something I was excited to add to my life, especially after what I had just gone through with Tasha. Jai told me she would understand if I needed to move on, but something kept telling me to hold on. It might have been God's will or my own desire to do something good for someone else, but I decided to stay with her and see things through.

The judicial system, or at least the one we encountered, was not what either of us was expecting. We pressed charges, but instead of Jai's ex having to go to court or trial, we were asked to go through mediation first and try to find a middle ground. It didn't make sense to either of us. He had broken the windows out of my truck and her house with bricks we'd seen him throw, but apparently, that didn't matter.

We showed up at the mediation hearing as instructed. The mediator sat down with the three of us and asked each of us to tell him what had happened. Jai went first. She explained how we had been in the kitchen when we'd first heard the noise of glass breaking and had ignored it until the brick had come flying through the front window. She described her point of view of the fight in the front yard and offered up the history of her relationships with me and her ex. The mediator turned to me and asked if there was anything I wanted to add.

"Nope," I said. "She got it all right. This motherfucker messed up her house. He's just lucky I didn't mess him up any more than I did," I said and sat back with my arms crossed.

The mediator raised his eyebrow a little at my comment and looked at his notes. He scribbled something down and turned to Jai's ex. "Okay, what happened from your point of view?"

He started his story by telling the mediator that he and Jai had been together off and on for a couple of years. I saw Jai shift in her chair as his lies started to multiply. He made up stories about their relationship and the feelings she had confessed to him. Jai tried to interrupt, but the mediator cut her off and reminded her that no one had interrupted her story. It was his turn to explain his side, and we would get a chance to dispute his story when he was done. Her ex continued spouting this fantasy. The more he spoke, the angrier I got. He finally got to the brick incident.

"I'm still not sure why this guy attacked me. I was out in the yard, just wanted to talk to Jai and try to win her back when this nigga ran out of the house and attacked me. I didn't even do anything," he said.

"The fuck you didn't," I screamed. "Don't come at me," I said, gesturing to Jai, "don't come at us with that bullshit. You know what you did. Quit fucking lying."

He didn't say anything else. The mediator put down his book and looked at the three of us. After a short pause, he let out a slight sigh. "Okay. So this isn't going to work," he said. "You guys are going to court."

The court hearing was in front of a judge. No jury and nothing like what you see on daytime TV with Judge Mathis. It was similar to the mediation, but this time, the judge would decide the outcome. We each presented our sides of the story, with me backing up Jai. Her ex began the same sob story he'd told the mediator, and it was clear right away that the judge was siding with him. I'm not sure if it was my appearance or what made her ex so believable, but there wasn't anything we could do to sway the judge back to our story and the facts.

In the end, the judge decided that Jai's ex would need to help us cover the deductible with the insurance company to pay for the damage he had caused, but only a portion. The total came to around $300. I was livid, and Jai was heartbroken. The whole reason we had decided to go forward with pressing charges was so that her ex would have some sort of consequence for his actions. After all of our time and energy, he got slapped with what equated to a $300 fine. No restraining order, no jail time, nothing but a light slap on the wrist. What was the point? We both knew we'd have to continue dealing with him on our own. The system had failed us.

Jai and I had been together for about a month by then. I had met her two kids from a previous guy, Mikayla and Scott, and we had introduced them to Sky. The three of them got along well, and I was starting to build a good relationship with them. I also realized by this point that Jai was the one. We would continue to have arguments and drama in our lives, but she was the woman I wanted to marry someday. We just had to figure out what to do about her ex.

He continued to come around and cause problems. It hadn't escalated to the point of throwing more bricks, but I knew that if he could do it once, he could do it again. Late one night, Jai confessed to me that she was worried about her safety and about the kids. She had seen her ex following them when I wasn't around. I was done. No one was going to mess with my family anymore.

I knew one of the guys that her ex hung out with. The next morning, I called him.

"Is this Mike?" I said.

"Yeah, who's this?" said the guy on the other end.

"This is Will. You're friends with a guy who's been causing me and my girl a lot of problems. I need you to give him a message for me."

I told him what had been going on between us and Jai's ex. He didn't say much until I had finished.

"Look, man. I don't support what he's doing, but he's still my friend," Mike said.

"I get that, and that's why I called you. Tell him that if I see him one more time, if he follows Jai or her kids, if I so much as hear that he's bothering any of them, I'm going to kill him."

"What?" Mike said.

"If he comes over here one more time, I am going to kill him."

There was silence for a while as Mike tried to figure out what to say. He finally responded, "Okay, Will. I get it. If he wants to ruin his life and die over a female, that's on him. You gotta do what you gotta do," and he hung up.

Jai's phone rang a little while later. She came into the living room, pale and with tears streaming down her cheeks.

"It's him, Will," she said. "He told me he's coming over right now."

I didn't say anything. I didn't need to. I kissed her forehead, took off my shirt, and grabbed the baseball bat we had near the front door.

He showed up down the block in his car a few minutes later, Mike in the passenger seat. I stood in the middle of the street, holding the bat in my right hand and bouncing it in my left. The sun beat down on my tattoo-covered chest and arms and reflected off of the snow on the ground. The sedan was parked about half a block away, running but not moving, both of them trying to figure out what to do next. I raised my left hand and motioned for them to come closer, but neither of them moved.

"Come on," I screamed. "Come on, motherfucker!" No movement from either of them. "I ain't got all day. This ends now. Come on, nigga. Let's end this. One of us is gonna die today!"

They both sat there, only their heads moving as they faced each other to talk. They were too far away, and the car's engine made too much noise for me to hear what they were saying, but I could guess. It felt like hours passed before they put the car in reverse and backed down the street. They pulled into a neighbor's driveway, turned around, and drove away. I went back inside and put the bat down. Jai hugged and kissed me harder than I had ever been kissed before.

"Is it over?" she asked, tears still on her cheeks.

"I think it's over," I said.

There comes a time when you have to take a stand—when someone pushes you too far. A time when you try to follow the rules and play the game the way society tells you to play it only to run out of time and options. My family, those I cared about more than anything else, even my own life, had been pushed too far, and it was up to me to put an end to it. I had to end the harassment, even if it meant that someone could get hurt or worse, but it had to end. Thankfully, for all of us, it did end that day. We never heard from Jai's ex again.

chapter 17

Jai and I got married, and life continued getting better. I kept my job at the post office working nights. She was employed, too, and our bills were getting paid. Most months, we even had a little extra to hold onto. Her kids started to call me dad and got along great with Sky. Our families started to blend, and for the first time in my life, I felt like everything was coming together. I had the family I'd always wanted. There were still some hard times, but there were so many more good times.

Jai's daughter, Mikayla, was great at basketball, and I started working with her to improve her skills when she was in eighth grade. By the time she was a junior in high school, I was helping her with her recruiting process for college. Hopefully, she could get some sort of scholarship and start on a better foot than I ever had.

Jai's son, Scott (nicknamed Day Day), loved to listen to the music I continued to work on. I wasn't in a group anymore, but I was still writing my own stuff and recording some solo songs. The continued advances in technology, especially in music production, allowed me to teach myself how to record and mix songs. I continued to talk with Axe and JD, but I didn't need their skills to put music together anymore. Most of what I recorded was similar to what was coming out each year by other R&B and rap artists. My songs focused on the streets and gangster life. I figured it was selling for other people, and it was what I knew.

The only ongoing issue was my work schedule. Working nights was fine when I didn't have anything to look forward to during the day or a family to help raise, but now it was more of a burden. I didn't mind working at the post office, but it wasn't my passion the way music was. I found myself missing my family and all the moments they were experiencing together. An incident with Sky put my priorities back in focus, and I knew I had to make a change as soon as possible. A day shift mail carrier position opened up, so I put in for it and ended up getting it.

Until then, I thought I was in pretty good physical shape. I worked out daily and had a pretty intimidating physique, but that hadn't prepared me for the cardio demands that delivering mail from house to house would require. The pain in my legs at the end of the first shift was almost unbearable. I thought they were going to fall off, and I remember telling Jai I didn't think I could keep going.

"After all you've been through, delivering mail is going to be the thing that lays you up?" she asked with a smirk.

"You don't get it," I told her. "I don't think I can *walk* anymore!"

"Well, baby, you're either going to need to find a new job or continue on. You can do this."

I got up the next morning, and my legs were on fire. I wanted to pass out, or at least stay in bed, but I knew I had to keep going. I had to give this job the best effort I could for my family. A few days went by, and my legs started getting better. After two weeks, most of the initial pain had subsided, and I thought I might be able to actually make this work long-term, but my manager seemed to have a different plan.

Her name was Karen, and it was evident from day one that she didn't like me. I still can't figure out what I'd done or what she thought she knew about me, but all she wanted to do was criticize my performance. She started following me from a distance on my daily routes and would write me up for even the slightest irregularity. Her harassment continued to build until one day, I had enough and blew up at her.

That was all she needed. She told me to get out of her office and called the inspector, her boss, to report me. I finished my shift because I didn't want to give her any more ammunition against me. The day ended, and I called Jai on my way home to tell her what was going on.

"I can't take it anymore. First it was my legs and knees. I fought through that because all I wanted was to have a normal life and provide for you. But this woman, she won't leave me alone. She harasses me every day, makes me feel incompetent. She hates me, Jai, and I'm not sure what I did. I lost my cool today. Blew up at her. I think I just lost my job."

The investigation into my actions started the next morning. With the union in place, they couldn't fire me without a formal review. The inspector started by interviewing me and my boss, then he went on to my coworkers. There wasn't anything I could do but wait for the end and the inspector's results. Everything was in his hands.

I went on my normal route, expecting a phone call informing me of my termination, but it never came. My phone didn't ring, and I completed my deliveries. All that was left was to head back to the office, drop off my stuff, and figure out whether I still had a job or not. The inspector was waiting for me when I arrived. He called me into Karen's office. She was already sitting there with her arms crossed, and she wasn't smiling. I sat down in the chair next to her.

The inspector explained that the investigation was over. After interviewing most of my team members, he had come to the conclusion that I had done nothing wrong. In fact, he said, I was performing above expectations, and I would be keeping my job. He told Karen that she needed to leave me alone, that almost all of my coworkers had reported some form of harassment from her on my behalf, and that it needed to end immediately. She was pissed and verbally attacked him, telling him his conclusion was bullshit. The glare she shot me let me know that she was going to make my life an even worse hell than it already was. I got up to say something to her, but the inspector told her to leave. She stormed out, and I sat back down.

"Man, you heard what everyone told you about her. What am I supposed to fucking do? I can't keep working like this!" I pleaded with him.

The inspector looked slightly defeated but put a hand on my shoulder. "Just calm down, Will. Do your job, and you'll be alright." I shook my head, knowing that he was full of it and nothing would change for the better.

I was right. The next week, she started to add houses to my route. It seemed like she found more work for me to do every single day. The write-ups had stopped, but now she was trying to destroy my will to work. Instead of firing me, she wanted me to quit, and there was no way I was going to let that happen. I kept going faster and working harder. Occasionally I'd fall, twist an ankle, or bang up my knee, but I had to keep going.

The only exception to my daily grind was a random mental health day here and there. I'd call in sick and just stay in bed all day. It was one of the few opportunities I would have to recover and let my body heal. I was incredibly careful those days because I didn't want to form a pattern or give her another excuse to put more work or pressure on me. Jai could always tell when I needed one of those days. My knees would start to get so bad, I could hardly walk. She'd start asking when I was going to take some time off and remind me that I needed to take care of myself or I'd end up on disability.

The pain continued to get worse. It spread from my knees to my lower back, starting with a dull pain that grew into a stabbing sensation. The stabbing intensified from tiny prickling pins to full-on knife blades. Even the mental health days were starting to become less effective in subsiding the constant pain.

Then a true blessing came—another station had an opening. I put in a bid to transfer that was approved, and I got a new manager and a new route. My workload decreased to a reasonable level, and my pain became more manageable. For a couple of months, everything was in a good place. I loved my new manager and the work I was doing. The people on my route started to recognize me and enjoyed the work ethic I had. Nothing could go wrong.

My deliveries became routine. I knew which houses had dogs that liked me and which didn't. The sidewalk wasn't the best, but I figured out which sections were particularly bad and required more attention than others. The miles I walked every day got easier with each step, and the pain in my knees and back was as good as it had been when I'd first started with the post office. I never expected my back would go out at the end of my shift one day.

Things started pretty normal. I picked up my letters and packages and parked my vehicle at the end of the street. There were still pretty constant aches and pains in my knees and lower back, but I had learned to deal with them. I popped a couple of ibuprofen and continued on my way. As I rounded the corner to deliver the last couple of items, I felt a sudden spasm, and pain ran from the middle of my back down to my toes. People had told me what it was like to have a back spasm, but until you experience it first-hand, you have no idea.

Everything locked up, and I fell to the ground, writhing in pain. For a moment, I just lay there, trying to figure out what was going on. I couldn't move anything because every time I did, a new dagger of pain would shoot along my spine. My legs lay in weird angles because of how the spasm had caused me to fall. After what I'm guessing was about ten minutes, the pain started to lessen, and I was able to bring myself to my knees. I called the station to let them know what had happened and finished my deliveries for the day.

I hobbled into the station and talked briefly with my boss. He told me I'd have to file for worker's comp since the incident happened on my route. The paperwork wasn't easy, but I got it done. The station told me to stay home, and the doctor got me some pain meds that helped me sleep. The post office didn't want to put me on disability. It would be an additional cost to them without any work from me. They had me get a note from my doctor that explained my diagnosis. My doctor had written it willingly and had explained to me what he'd seen on my X-rays, but it wasn't enough. They sent me to their doctor for a second opinion. We went back and forth for more than a month, them trying to prove I was lying or that my pain was a pre-existing condition. After seeing numerous specialists, they finally gave in and put me on disability.

By this time, I starting to go crazy being stuck at home with nothing to do except deal with the pain in my back. It was getting manageable, but I knew there was no way I could go back to work without hurting myself again. All the time off without anything to keep me busy started to lead my mental health down a bad path again. My thoughts focused on all the negatives. Every time it seemed like things were finally going to come together in my life, another curveball, another bump in the road, was thrown my way. So far, I had been able to rise above it, but I wasn't sure how much more I could take.

The doctors put me on certain restrictions and told me I could return to work, but the post office wanted me to find another job. There wasn't anything available that matched my restrictions, and they didn't want to pay me if I wasn't working. I didn't blame them. My boss recommended me for a work rehabilitation program so I could figure out what to do next and get me off of their payroll sooner rather than later.

The first thing the program manager asked me was what I wanted to do. I didn't know how to answer the question. No one had ever asked me what I wanted. They had either judged me by my appearance or simply stayed out of my way. I told him I wasn't sure, and he explained that the program could help me find a new path. It was almost overwhelming to have someone tell me I could make this kind of change in my life without any pretense. He left me with my thoughts and came back a while later.

"I want to be a social worker," I announced when he came back in. The shock he tried to conceal told me this was not the answer he'd expected.

"What kind of social worker?" he asked.

"I've lived a rough life," I told him. "I want to help kids before they make the choices I did. I want to share my story so they don't end up going down the same path. If I can show them that someone else cares, that there is someone they can trust, then maybe I can make a difference."

His shock changed to curiosity, and then to a slight smile. "I think I have just the person you need to talk to," he said.

After a couple of phone calls, I met with a guy named Jeremy who was the director of ManUp Iowa. He explained that the mission and vision of the organization was to empower at-risk young men, specifically in the Des Moines metro, with limited resources to reach adulthood successfully. It sounded like what I was looking for, and he brought me on as a mentor. The money wasn't the best, but I could do the work and finally make a difference.

Shortly after I'd signed on to the program, Jeremy left, and a new guy took the reins. It was pretty clear from the beginning that he was a little iffy about me. He wasn't sure about my looks or my approach with the kids. I was a big, intimidating black guy with tattoos and a durag covering a scarred-up head. Would I really be able to connect with the kids, or would I scare them off with my appearance before they could even get into the program? It felt like I was already falling into the same cycle of mild success followed by failure due to circumstances beyond my control.

The new Executive Director was great at administration and paperwork. He knew how to get grants and how to make sure the organization was running like a clock behind the scenes. As soon as possible, I showed him I could connect with the kids and get them interested in what we were doing. We did a couple of presentations at East High School on East 13th Street just off the interstate. The kids loved my presentation and the rawness of the story I brought about my life experience in Chicago. The parents appreciated it as well. They couldn't get their kids to listen to them, but I could. They believed in my message, and they turned to us for help.

The program started to grow as more kids came in for guidance and support. The ED and I still didn't get along, but we appreciated each other's strengths and tried to keep out of each other's way. The most important thing was that the kids who needed help were getting it.

Throughout this transitional period, I kept doing music and writing songs. There was still a gangster side in me, and my music showed that. It let me express myself in ways that I couldn't at work or with my family. Most of the songs centered around violence and sex, mirroring what was popular in the music industry. It had never occurred to me that my music could do anything or be anything different than what I was hearing on the radio, but that would all change the evening of June 9, 2015.

chapter 18

Death had become something I was used to by this point in my life. I had seen so many friends and gangsters die one way or another growing up that it seemed normal. Every day, the news reported another shooting in another neighborhood, and someone else I didn't know dying too young. Occasionally, it was a black kid shooting another black kid in a bad drug deal or a fight over a girl. More often, it was simply a senseless act of violence that could have been prevented if someone would have listened or would have been willing to help a kid make a better choice. It was what it was, and there didn't seem to be a way to break the cycle.

That all changed on the evening of June 9. My son was hanging out in his room when he got a phone call from one of his friends. A few minutes later, he came out shaken and on the verge of tears. Terry Harris, his best friend, who my son and nephew were supposed to be hanging out with, had been shot and killed by another kid. The kid had shot him in his own room in front of his little brother. My children were devastated, and I was angry. What the hell was going on? Why would anyone want to shoot this kid? I sat there in silence, tears falling from my eyes.

A silent and confusing week went by. All of us were trying to come to terms with what had happened, but none of us knew what to say or how to help one another. Terry's death didn't make sense, but there didn't seem to be anything we could do. Late one afternoon, I was watching TV in the living room by myself when my son, daughter, and nephew rushed in, all talking at the same time. Through the confusion, I could tell they were asking me to do something about Terry's death.

"What do you want me to do?" I said, still angry and confused.

"Write a song. Quit doing songs about sex and put out something about what is going on in the community. Tell our story, tell Terry's story, tell people what is happening here."

Their words hit me so hard, it felt like someone had knocked the wind out of me. It shocked me. I had no idea they had that kind of confidence in me or in my voice. All of the other songs I had been working on disappeared, and I knew this was something I had to do. I had to tell a story and tell it my way. No sugar-coating, no mincing words. This was going to be real and raw. I had to wake people up to the reality of what was happening in their own neighborhoods. Terry's story had to be told.

The kids and I talked a little more, and then I went to my studio. I needed to focus and figure out what this song was going to be. It started with the beat. Once I had that locked down, the lyrics started to flow. People had to know what was happening, what these kids were doing, and how we might be able to come together to make it better.

Creating music is a mysterious process. Putting together meaningful words out of nothing, and a beat and a tune to accompany them, can be an overwhelming task. There have been times when writer's block kept me paralyzed for days, if not weeks, as I tried to come up with the next lyric or chord, but that didn't happen with this song. It only took a couple of days. My motivation and new sense of purpose opened up a creative side of me that I hadn't known was there. I recorded a rough take and had my kids and nephew come listen to it. They loved it immediately. That was the birth of the song, "Wake Up Iowa," and the ember that sparked the Starts Right Here Movement, my personal advocacy program.

I took the recording to the ED over at ManUp. To me, it made perfect sense to include this in what we were trying to do with youth in Des Moines and the state of Iowa. ManUp was starting to get a little more recognition, and I wanted to help the organization continue to reach more kids. This raw type of track that spoke the honest truth was what kids and parents had been telling me they wanted to hear. Who knew how many we might be able to help?

"We're not going to play that. It's terrible," he said after listening to "Wake Up Iowa" for the first time. "This is going to hurt the organization, and it's going to hurt your career, Will. I think you should just forget about this."

His reaction stunned me. I left his office not sure what was going on or why he'd had such a visceral reaction. It didn't make any sense. That night, I told my kids what had happened, and they told me to make use of the track and make a music video anyway, that I didn't need his approval to do this on my own time.

They were right. I knew I had to get this out.

I had already done a couple of music videos for some of my other songs, but I wanted this one to be different. It needed to be professionally done, and it needed to have the right mix of people involved. One of the first calls I made was to the former white supremacist, Frank Meeink. Frank was the inspiration for Edward Norton's character in *American History X*. We had met through my sister-in-law, and he had taken an interest in my work and music. When I told him about the song and the video, he immediately jumped on board to direct and organize it. He explained that he had a concept for a video he had been sitting on, and that this was the opportunity he had been waiting for. His concept wasn't exactly what I had in mind, but having his notoriety and support could make a huge impact on the reach of the final product. So I told him okay.

The next call was to Pastor Al Perez, who had become a mentor of mine through our connection with ManUp Iowa. We talked about everything from the kids we were mentoring to family issues to general life. I shared my vision, and he volunteered to assist me in any way he could. He helped me find actors, and his connections and relationships with the police department were integral to my early success in building those relationships. I worked with Quincey King, a local rap artist, to sing with me and round out the harmonies. Everything was set.

After explaining how we wanted to reach the troubled youth community, we got access to the Polk County Jail to film the prison scenes. It was the first music video to ever be shot on location in the prison. Frank and I continued to have arguments on the concept, and some outside family issues started demanding more from him. He wasn't able to devote the amount of time or energy needed to put together the video I was hoping to release. We continued filming, and I continued working with my other partners because we had to get this out, if for no other reason than I had told my kids I would do it.

We wrapped filming and got the video edited. It wasn't perfect, and it didn't have the message I was hoping for, but it was done. The only thing left to do was upload it to various social media platforms and hold my breath.

It took off on Facebook first. The Des Moines police department was the most influential group to originally share it. The message of cooperation and community-building resonated with their whole department, and they wanted to show support for what we were trying to do. YouTube views started to rise, and some of the local news stations picked it up. Unknown numbers started showing up on my cell phone from reporters wanting to sit down with me and hear the story of the video. The interviews started, and my message resonated with even more people. More phone calls and interviews came, but this time, they wanted to hear my story, not only my reasons for the video. Suddenly, I had a voice in the community. People were starting to hear my name and know who Will Keeps was, and they wanted more.

The chief of the Des Moines police department, Dana Wingert, called to tell me how much the department appreciated all I was doing and saying. They had never experienced anything like this before, and they wanted to make sure we continued to work together. I got invited to a church ceremony where they wanted to show the video to the congregation and hear me speak. As the video began, I could see people were apprehensive, but I took the mic after it was over, and by the end of my speech, people were standing and applauding, wanting even more. A woman approached me as I was leaving the church and asked if I would consider doing a video about police violence and what was happening in the black community.

"I don't know," I told her. "I'm not sure if that's my stage or my message."

"It most certainly is, Will. You need to share this message like you did with 'Wake Up Iowa.' People need to know what's going on and hear the naked truth, not just what the news says."

She persisted a little more, and I told her I would do it, though I wasn't sure what exactly *it* was.

There seemed to be support for me almost everywhere I went, except the one place I hoped would support me the most. The week after the video went viral, the ED at ManUp had some words for me.

"What are you doing, Will?" he asked one afternoon after the kids had gone home for the night. He was angry, but I didn't know why.

"What do you mean?" I asked, slightly taken aback.

"This video, the news shows…I told you when you made that song that it wasn't going to be good for you or ManUp Iowa, but you did it anyway. Now it seems like you're working on that stuff more than you're doing your job here."

"Man, we have more kids coming into the program, and I'm still making sure I'm covering everything you ask me to do. I'm doing this video and all the other things on my own time. Besides, this has been great for ManUp."

"Has it, Will?" he asked.

I didn't know what to say, so I stood there for a second, gathering my thoughts. "Yeah, it really has," I said finally, sticking to my guns. "And I'm working on another video that I think will generate even more publicity for what we're doing here."

"What we're doing?" he asked as he raised an eyebrow at me.

"Yeah, what we're building. I thought we were going to be partners and make this organization great."

"We're not partners, Will. I'd rather you be an employee, not my partner," the ED said in a monotone voice as he walked away.

A new guy started the following Monday. I found out that he was my new boss, someone to watch over me and deal with me so the ED wouldn't have to. Though it was never said out loud, it was implied many times that the ED didn't like what I was doing and that I was getting more attention than ManUp was. Other things started to change. I was stripped from all marketing materials and promotional engagements. There was nothing about me on the tables or brochures. The organization was doing well and growing because of the engagement and connections I had established with the black community, but from the outside looking in, I didn't exist. It didn't help that I learned my new boss was also getting paid $5 an hour more than I was to keep me in check. Although I wanted to keep my relationships and the impact I was having on my community, I wasn't sure that ManUp was the right place for me anymore.

Over the next few weeks, I continued to work on the song that the woman at the church had requested. It didn't come as easy as "Wake Up Iowa" had, but when it was done, I was happy with it. Police Chief Wingert and I had started to build a friendship, so I called him and asked if he'd listen to my next song and the concept I was working on for the video. He met me at my house that same afternoon, and by the time we were done, he asked if he could be in the video. I was shocked.

"This video could be the start of the change we need to make, Will," he told me. "I want to be a part of that change."

We talked through our schedules and got some filming dates on the calendar. As he was leaving, I said, "You know, Chief, if we do this, some people are gonna love us, but a lot more are gonna hate us. I'm still getting hate for 'Wake Up Iowa.'"

I told him about how when the video had first taken off, it had seemed like everyone loved it and that there was nothing but support. But I explained how that had died down pretty quickly. Active gangsters and kids looking to join gangs in and around Des Moines felt like I was talking down to them and diminishing them. They told me I had lost my edge and that they were harder than I'd ever been back in Chicago.

I'd stood my ground, and tried to make them understand that they didn't really want the gangster lifestyle coming into their neighborhoods. One of the best methods was to ask questions like, "When you walk outside your house, what do you see?" Their answers were almost always the same: "I see houses, cars, trees, grass," whatever. So I'd tell them, "I wish that was all I'd seen back in Chicago. When I walked outside my house, I saw gangsters, I saw crackheads, I saw prostitutes, I saw guns. I'm not saying there are no gangsters in Iowa, but there's a limit to them. When you walk outside your house, the fire, the street, isn't right there. You have to go look for the fire and bring it back to your home, and why would you want to do that? Why would you want to bring the fire to your neighborhood when it's not there?" No one had an answer to that question and that's why I knew this new song and video were going to work. We were going to get right in their faces and show them the danger they were trying to bring home.

The Chief took it all in and sat for less than a second with the story I'd told him. "I don't care, Will. I like what you're saying, I like the concept, and I want to be a part of it," he said.

We finalized the shooting dates, shook hands, and I went back to my studio to work on a final cut. Later that same day, I had my second community song finalized, and "We Fight" was ready to move into video production.

The day before the shoot, the Chief called and told me he had to reschedule. In his line of work, things like this were pretty common. I told him I understood, and we got it on the calendar a few days later. The reschedule placed the shoot during one of my mentorship times. I didn't want to sneak around behind the ED's or my new boss's back, so I called them and told them what was going on.

"Will, this is getting ridiculous. This is exactly what I was worried about. Your priorities are getting way out of whack right now. It seems like you care more about this video than you do the kids we're trying to help. Maybe it's time you took a break from ManUp for a while."

He had gone too far. I had helped build this program and had gotten it to a new level. In his mind, he thought that ManUp was my only avenue to helping kids in the community. He had no right to accuse me of misplacing my priorities.

The words came out faster than I could think them. "You know, man, when we first got together, I thought we could be a great team. I thought we could partner on this and make ManUp Iowa bigger than either of us ever realized. Then you hired a manager for me and made it clear you just wanted a bitch-ass employee. So no, I don't think it's time for me to take a break. I'll do you one better. I quit." With that, I hung up the phone.

Leaving ManUp felt like a weight had been lifted from my shoulders. I didn't hold any ill will against the ED, and to this day, I still hope he's succeeding. He taught me a lot about the nonprofit world and how to successfully build an organization. We may not have always seen eye-to-eye, and it turned out we were never meant to be partners, but I know he wanted to help kids as much as I did. We just had different ways of reaching that goal.

We shot the "We Fight" video, and it was true to my concept. Everything I wanted for this video was happening. The Chief was in it from the beginning and wanted it to be as raw and as real as I did. As we wrapped up filming, I was confident we had something revolutionary and inspirational on our hands. All it needed now was editing and final production before we could launch.

I never did find out how, but the press got wind that we were putting together another video. A black ex-gangster partnering with the Chief of Police to raise public awareness of violence toward the black community was unheard of. They wanted to know what was going on, when the video was going to be released, who was involved, and why this had even happened in the first place. Chief Wingert and I decided that we needed to get ahead of the speculation and rumors, so we set up an interview with KCCI, a local news station, to answer questions directly. The interview went better than expected, and they did a nice job portraying what we were doing and why.

No one can prepare you for when a viral moment happens. I had always dreamed of being famous, being in front of a crowd, and having a stage I could perform on. That innocent seven-year-old kid in the Spider-Man pajamas, the college guy alone on a stage in front of his peers during a talent show, the group member who had a shot to sing with Mary J. Blige, and the guy putting together songs and music videos to make a difference in his community all had the same drive—they wanted to be known. That old saying, "be careful what you wish for," could not have been more prophetic.

After the interview aired, the local stations all started talking about my upcoming music video and my unprecedented partnership with law enforcement. Clips from "Wake Up Iowa" were picked up and played on loops through primetime broadcasts. CNN picked it up, and I started to get calls from friends and journalists from all over the country. People in Las Vegas, California, and New York all wanted to know when "We Fight" was coming out and how they could get an exclusive.

Other stories started to break as the twenty-four/seven/three-sixty-five news media machine started looking for an edge, something they could use to get more views. People I'd never heard of were leaving me messages, sending me DMs, or trying to figure out who I was and what I was doing. The most-asked question: "Where's the damn video?" The problem was, I didn't have it ready.

The questions got more intense as people wanted to see something that didn't exist. People started to talk on various social media channels, losing their confidence that I'd be able to get it out, saying that I was just trying to continue to ride my fifteen minutes of fame from "Wake Up Iowa." The opinions from haters didn't bother me. I didn't know any of them, so why should I care what they thought? At this point, I wanted to get the video out more than anyone, but I also knew that it had to be perfect. There wasn't going to be another shot. Once it was out, that was it.

The anticipation continued to build, and so did the pressure. It hit a high point when one of the main headlines was shared on World-Star, a social media site for hip hop with a mostly black audience. There was some early support, but that quickly changed as more and more people started attacking me and my motives. Cheap insults turned into harsh charges of me being a racist or a coon, playing up stereotypes to support a white agenda. Someone called me an Uncle Tom, meaning I was growing subservient to white ways and forgetting my black culture.

Insults and negativity continued to flow from people who didn't understand the connections I was trying to make or why I was working to build partnerships with the police. I was scared of these reactions because I never wanted the black community to go against me, especially on something as important as this. There was far more praise and positivity, but I couldn't get past the three to five percent who were extremely negative. Their comments and insults stuck in my brain and kept me awake at night. My wife and cousin told me to quit reading the inflammatory posts and let my work speak for itself, but I kept on consuming stupid opinions.

At first, the comments and insults made me feel weak and hopeless, but as I continued reading, I was hit with a realization. These people didn't know me, or my intentions, or what I'd been through to motivate me to finish this project. A lot of people will give up on an idea or goal if they receive even a little negative feedback. If one or two people push back, they throw in the towel and go back to what they know. It's easier to give up and stay safe doing what you've always done, but I couldn't. This message and the mission were too important to be stopped by negativity from strangers behind computer screens. I turned their negativity from weakness into strength.

If they didn't like what I was doing or saying, that must mean I was doing something right, and I wasn't about to stop.

The comments continued, but I knew I could deal with them. I decided to respond to a particularly nasty one because I wanted to see why the guy was hating on me so much. He had called me almost every name in the book and told me that my videos were trash. I asked him what he hated about my message that made him so angry. We went back and forth a couple times as I explained my mission. After a couple of exchanges, a message I never expected came through.

"You know what, Will? A lot of what you say makes sense. I didn't see it before, but I'm gonna give you a shot. I wanna see what you can do. It's clear to me you're dead serious about what you're doing, so I'm going to listen. Don't let me down."

It turns out, I didn't. The guy still listens to my music and encourages me to keep going to this day.

That was all I needed to see. I was able to change one person's mind. If I could do that once, maybe I could do it again. Maybe all the late nights, negative comments, and stress of going against the grain would be worth it. God was working on me to see what I could handle. Would I run and hide, or would I stand up and continue to fight to move this idea forward?

"We Fight" came out of production completely perfect. It had everything I'd wanted for "Wake Up Iowa" and so much more. We made the announcement that it was done and dropped it on social media. It went viral almost immediately—100,000 views in the first couple of hours and more than a million views combined on the various social channels. It seemed like it was getting played everywhere. I couldn't have asked for a better initial reception, and neither could the Chief.

As we all know, there's incredible capacity for good in social media. Without it, I wouldn't have the voice that I do today. But there's also a darker side, and the two are not mutually exclusive.

The Chief of Police and I both started receiving incredible praise for "We Fight," but we also received severe criticism. It got to the point that he called me one afternoon and told me we had to do something. He was taking so much heat and getting beat up from all sides. We needed to get together and emphasize our message of togetherness and community-building.

We did another interview with the local news and explained how we could work together, that the police force and the black community didn't have to be enemies. In fact, by working alongside each other, we could build stronger, safer, and more inclusive neighborhoods. There didn't have to be sides, and it didn't need to be us versus them. It could be all of us working together to make sure we left our city better than we'd found it.

People still pushed back. This idea of togetherness and inclusivity was foreign to them, and they couldn't comprehend why we would want to work together. But for every naysayer, there were at least a hundred supporters pushing us forward and telling us to continue the work we started. They gave both of us strength, especially me. Whenever I felt like it was overwhelming, or that I couldn't find the will to put up with the name-calling, I'd turn to the support and remind myself why we were doing this work. So many people had thought that I was going to simply be a one-hit-wonder and disappear. They'd all underestimated me. I was in it for the long haul, and I needed to see this through in whatever form it took.

chapter 19

I knew my work wasn't done, I just wasn't sure where I was supposed to be going. The videos and songs I was putting out were my passion, and they were starting to gain a lot of renown not only in Des Moines, but nationwide. The problem was, the music didn't pay the bills. The money for filming, editing, and production was coming out of my pocket. A donor or sponsor would occasionally help with a portion of the cost, but it wasn't nearly enough for me to make a living and take care of my family. My wife and I started fighting over money and the time I was spending on my projects. It got so bad, we almost split at one point. I knew I needed to make a change, but I wasn't sure what I was being called to do. I didn't want to give up on all the good that was happening, but I also couldn't keep blindly spending money I didn't have to keep it afloat. Something needed to change. I needed to start something new.

My cousin suggested I reach out to the schools directly and see if there was anything I could offer. Maybe a class or a mentoring program could help me pay the bills while I worked with the kids who needed my message the most. He also told me that I really needed to look at starting a non-profit. I knew what it was like to work for a non-profit, but I had no idea how to start one. Still, his words remained in the back of my mind. Maybe I could establish an organization that might make a lasting impact, but where do I begin?

Luckily, around that same time, Des Moines Public Schools called. They found out I wasn't with ManUp Iowa anymore and wanted to know if I could come in and do a mentoring session with some of their most at-risk youth. I told them this was the call I had been waiting for, the call I didn't know I needed. They had made my dreams come true, and if I could, if the kids needed me, I would do it all day long.

The district hired me and brought me in to work with the high school kids no one else could get through to. The kids that weren't used to structure or having anyone to listen or look up to. The few who did have a support system weren't using it. They were the ones the system would soon leave behind. The ones who would likely end up on the street before having a chance to graduate and seek better opportunities. They needed help the most, but they were the least likely to accept it. They were me on the South Side of Chicago, so many years ago.

It started off kind of slow with a few kids who took a chance on me. Those initial kids then told others that I was different. I wasn't the normal educator who was doing this thing for a couple of years to earn some forgiveness on their student loans and move along. I told stories, spoke their language, and offered them the truth. There weren't any empty threats or sugar-coating; my message was real, and it was raw. Word of the program got out, and more kids wanted to be a part of it. They wanted to be mentored.

It wasn't just the fact that kids were showing up, it was that they wanted to be there. This wasn't about compliance because no one was requiring them to attend. These kids craved growth and a second chance. There were kids from opposing gangs, kids who were racist and hated each other, but we never had a fight break out. We had arguments, but we also had respect, and the respect always won out. To have a room full of these young people listen and respect not only each other, but also the person at the front of the room, was a breakthrough.

Someone from school administration heard about the success of my program. It wasn't every day a guy could have ongoing growth with the hardest cases in the district. They reached out to me and told me they wanted to start a more permanent program at SCAVO, an alternative school within the Des Moines Public Schools system. I met with a few influential administrators, and we put together a program that would run alongside the regular school year.

We worked through the summer and determined the objectives of this pilot program. One afternoon near the end of summer, I was sitting on the front porch of my home in Des Moines when it hit me. I wanted to do something memorable that would capture these kids' attention immediately. They had already gone through so much and had experienced more than the average person would in a lifetime. They had seen and heard everything and had been told about the advantages of education and why they needed to stick to school by people who had never walked in their shoes. The pandering hadn't worked and never would because most of the people mentoring these kids didn't know what it was like to have a gun drawn on them or to buy drugs on the street. But I did, and these kids needed to know it from the beginning. But how?

I took a deep breath and looked around. The answer hit me like a ton of bricks. Sitting on my own porch, I was taken back to the front porch of my childhood home in Chicago. The smell of the asphalt and the heat reminded me of the good times I'd had there with my brother, sister, and friends, the conversations we'd had and the community we were building until the influence of the street and the drugs crept their way into my life. I had learned so much on that porch, and it was my personal safe space. That was the program I wanted to build. A place where these kids could feel safe, where they could have open and honest conversations without the worry or judgement of the outside world. We needed a porch.

The summer came to an end, and we put the building blocks in place for the launch of the program. To say I was scared was an understatement. I was trying something completely new, and I didn't want it to fail. I worked to manage my self-doubt about whether or not any kids would even sign up. Most of the kids I was trying to reach had already had mentors or counselors work with them, and none of those experiences had worked. If they had, they wouldn't be looking into my program. I also knew that for most of the kids who would walk through my door, it was their last chance. If this didn't work, they'd end up on the streets, in jail, or dead. That's a heavy weight to bear.

The one thing I had going for me from the beginning was my music. Through the partnerships with the police department and the success of "We Fight" and "Wake Up Iowa," the kids knew who Will Keeps was. They respected my music, and they wanted to find out more about me. We opened the program, and twenty kids enrolled right away. Like my previous program, there was respect almost immediately. There were occasional issues, but the kids knew I was actually there to help them, not just talk at them.

The first semester ended on a pretty high note. My program got renewed for another semester, and we enrolled another twenty kids or so. I felt like I was connecting, and my work to bring the community together, or at least save a few kids, was taking root. Then I got the call I had been fearing since I first became a mentor. One of my kids from the program had been shot and killed.

It had been a senseless act of gun violence and was in and out of the news in less than twenty-four hours. But it left a hole in me. It made me want to go harder and be even more aggressive with my role in these kids' lives. I didn't want to be a passive advocate for them. They had to know I was not only there to mentor them, but to protect them. I cared about their feelings and their lives outside of my porch program.

I started working on another song called "Starts Right Here." The song and video focus on a young man who watches his mom get killed during a botched robbery. His father continues to raise him, but takes on extra work in order to support his family. He's a good man and trusts his son to do the right thing while he's away. As the video goes on, the father notices that his son's grades are slipping and he starts hanging out with a group of kids that aren't a good influence. They get into a fight and the son storms out. Later that night, the son takes the father's gun and goes to a house party where he gets into another fight and pulls the gun on another kid. It's at this point that the memory of his mom dying in the robbery flashes before his eyes, and he stops in his tracks, frozen in fear. You'll have to watch the video to find out how it ends.

My hope for the song was to raise awareness of common issues within the black community. Issues I had gone through and been a part of in Chicago. The cycle of violence, fear, and distrust of the police department, escalation and more violence, and so on. One murder or drug deal gone wrong might result in another and another if no one steps forward and says, "enough is enough." The community continues to stick to the code of an eye for an eye and no one wants to be labeled a snitch. Add the rhetoric of bad cops and racial injustice around the country, and it's no wonder why so many black kids continue to die senseless deaths. I wanted to stop it, or at the very least, start a different conversation.

The Des Moines Police Department seemed to have me on speed dial. Anytime they couldn't get through to a teenager or a family when they were trying to solve a murder case in the black community, I got a call. People would talk to me, they respected me, and they knew I was trying to do right by them. They trusted me because I was one of them, and they knew I wasn't going to turn my back on them. This was what we needed more than any march or any protest. We needed actual action taken at our local level to build relationships and trust between people who were hurting and those who could help.

More kids enrolled in the program. More than my words, they knew from the songs and videos I was putting out and my actions that I cared about them. I was becoming an authority figure for them, someone who didn't only talk a good game, but backed it up when it mattered. Some of the kids even told me they would only go to school if I was there and asked me not to take any time off. They needed me, and I needed them to need me.

The program kept growing, and so did my ongoing relationships with the kids. There were a handful who truly excelled and did things I could only dream. Others made it through and ended up graduating middle-of-the-road. These kids were some of my favorites because had they not enrolled with me, society would have left them behind, dooming them to the streets and an early death. Then there were the ones who did die.

It was inevitable that not all of the kids in my program would make it out alive. Their lives and experiences prior to enrolling had already done too much damage. I wanted to inspire and help them change their direction, but that wasn't always possible. We lost a few more kids over the years, and each one destroyed me. But nothing would prepare me for the two-week period where I lost three individuals without warning. One young lady got shot over a drug deal gone wrong on a Tuesday. Two days later, a young man in my program, who I thought was on the verge of a major change, ended up also getting shot because of drugs. Then the next week, one my best friends in New York fell asleep at the wheel, hit a truck, and died instantly.

I wanted to quit. I wanted to walk away and find something else. It was too hard. There was too much loss, too much pain, and I wasn't sure if any of my actions were actually making a difference. If they were, why were people still dying? I wanted to save everyone, and if I wasn't able to, I was failing.

My daughter, Sky, and I had a conversation, and I told her I wanted to quit.

"Quit being selfish, Dad," she said.

"What are you talking about?" I asked, half upset. "How am I being selfish? I'm doing the best I can, and kids are still dying or walking away and giving up."

"Yeah, Dad, they are. But these kids need you. I know you're hurting right now, and I know it's not easy for you. You want to save everyone, but not everyone wants to be saved. If you walk away, if you quit because some of these kids don't want to be saved, you're just being selfish."

Not everyone wanted to be saved…

I hadn't considered my daughter's revelation. I'd been trying to save everyone, but I was never going to be able to because, in the end, the kids still had to make their own choice. I couldn't save them all, but I had to be there for the ones who wanted saving.

This thirty-second conversation lit a fire deep inside me and drove me harder. My programs expanded from high school to middle school and finally to elementary. I wanted to catch the kids younger, at a time when I could make an even bigger impact on their lives. Each building, each grade, required a different version of Will Keeps. In elementary, I had to be stern but fun and make it a game. Middle school required me to be more stern, but the kids had to like me. Otherwise, they wouldn't make the connection or give me a chance. High school was the hardest because not only did they have to like me, they had to respect me. It was the only way to influence their decision-making and put them on a different path. But the common thread through all of my programming was the music. They all loved it and craved to be a part of it. Most thought I was a local celebrity and simply wanted a shot to hear me talk or be in a music video.

More and more kids were enrolling each semester. I thought everything was on track, but I realized there were some barriers in the way schools had to be run that I would never be able to overcome. The kids were getting served, but in the back of my mind, I knew there was a better way to reach more kids and make a bigger impact if we could get past all the red tape and bureaucracy. Turns out, I wouldn't have to make that decision. After four years of continued growth and success, some of my programs weren't renewed, and I could see the writing on the wall. The current version of my program wasn't going to be around much longer. What they didn't know, and what I didn't know, was that I was about to change the whole game in education.

chapter 20

I had never forgotten my cousin's words: "Will, you need to start a non-profit." I couldn't shake his suggestion and the idea of starting an organization to teach kids the way I knew they needed to be taught. With the school district cutting my program, it was time for me to act. But first, I needed a name.

My wife and I started brainstorming ideas. All kinds of names were thrown out, but none of them fit with what I wanted to build. We had a trip to Vegas coming up to see my father, and I really wanted to have a name before we got back to Iowa. On the flight to Vegas, we were talking through music videos, hoping to find a name. Ideas like "Wake Up Iowa" and some others were mentioned and quickly dismissed.

Jai turned to me and in a matter-of-fact way said, "Why don't you just name it Starts Right Here?" almost like the answer had been in front of us the entire time.

"That might work!" I yelled so loudly that everyone on the plane turned and looked at me at the same time. The attention caught me off guard, and I buried my face in my chest unable to hide the giant smile. Jai just shook her head and, after a brief pause, muttered, "Why?" under her breath.

We landed back in Iowa, and I started to work on the foundation of the organization. A board of directors was established along with by-laws for the newly formed non-profit. The mission was clear to me. We needed to help enable kids to graduate high school. Up to this point in my career, I had done this mainly through mentorship. During a discussion with my board, one of them suggested I actually open a school. I remember laughing and telling him, "Man, I ain't no Lebron James. I can't just open a school!"

"Why not?" he asked.

I didn't have a good response, and that made me realize that he was right. This couldn't just be another mentorship program. The community needed a school. One that was accessible, especially to at-risk kids who were on the verge of dropping out or had already. I needed a space to hold classes, and I needed some guidance and assistance to ensure the education we were offering would allow the kids to officially graduate. Starts Right Here was going to be more than another non-profit that helped troubled kids. We were going to build something that would change their lives. I wanted to give these kids another chance and help them graduate. I also wanted to show them that the community could come together, and that we could build something that made a difference and bridge the gaps between color, class, and more. Having that kind of dream and goal meant that I needed to have some pretty powerful people in my corner, so why not start at the top?

One of my buddies, David, was in security and saw what I was doing. The message resonated with him, and he wanted to help by introducing me to some people. I took him up on his offer. He told me I needed to meet this guy named Adam Gregg, an up-and-comer in the Iowa political scene who was connected to the Lt. Governor. Who was I to pass up this opportunity?

Now, I need to make something clear from the beginning, if for no other reason than to prove a point later on. I'm a registered Democrat and have been for my entire life. Adam was and is connected to some of the highest-profile Republicans in the state and the nation. I could have let our partisan politics detour me from taking the meeting with him. I could have turned my back and said, "Now why would he want to help another bleeding-heart, black Democrat?" But I didn't because what I was building was bigger than party and bigger than politics. This idea, Starts Right Here, was more than right-versus-left or conservative-versus-liberal. It was for everyone, and the community needed it. I felt so strongly about the mission and purpose that I knew I could make people from both parties see beyond their agendas. At the very least, I had to try because if I couldn't, the entire mission was doomed to fail. If I couldn't get leaders from both sides of the aisle to buy in, there wasn't any point in moving forward.

Adam and I hit it off immediately, and I knew I wanted to keep in touch with him. Around the same time, David introduced me to Lt. Governor Kim Reynolds. I didn't know what exactly I was going to say or how I was going to say it, but I knew I needed her support. When we were first introduced, I felt strongly in my gut that I was going to get to know this woman and that we were going to do big things for our community together. We talked briefly, and I told her my story and shared my ideas. She told me she was on board and wanted to talk more, but needed a little more time with everything going on in the state. I told her I understood and made sure to connect with her people to get something on the calendar.

After some follow-up, we set another meeting for March of 2017. I talked Dana Wingert, Al Perez, and a few other individuals into coming with me. My goal for the meeting was to get her to be in my upcoming music video for a new song called "Droppin.'"

"You're kind of pushing it, aren't you?" one of the police officers in the room said.

"Why not?" I replied. "Worst thing she can say is no."

At the capitol, we entered her office, and she had a huge smile on her face. She was genuinely happy to see me, and she cut right to the point.

"How can I help you, Will?" she asked.

I started to tell her my entire story as quickly as I could. This was my chance, and I didn't want to blow it by talking too much. I told her about the kids I wanted to help, the molestation when I was little, my life coming up in the streets and joining a gang, and what I wanted to do in Des Moines to save other children from going through what I'd endured. Tears started to fall down my face, and then she started to tear up. I looked around the room and almost everyone had a tear in their eye. I composed myself and went for it.

"You asked me how you can help me?" I asked. She nodded in affirmation. "I want you in my music video for a new song I'm putting out. With the crime rising in our community, I want some big leaders backing up what we're doing. I want to show the world that black, white, Republican, Democrat, rich, poor, privileged, not, doesn't matter. That we can work together and make this community better."

She asked to hear the song, so I played it for her. As the music faded, I looked at her one more time, knowing this was the moment of truth.

She smiled and said, "I'm in." I wanted to jump up and hug her, but I knew we didn't have that type of relationship yet. "When do you film?" she asked.

"Well, that's the problem. We're filming in three days," I started. "But we'll only need you for about an hour, and we can work to accommodate your schedule."

"Don't worry about accommodating me. I want to be in this," she said and motioned to her assistant. "Clear my schedule of whatever I have going on in three days. This is where I want to be."

The shoot came, and she was there the entire time. She didn't end up leaving until we had basically wrapped up filming. We ended up having the Chief of Police, the Lt. Governor, the Chief of Des Moines Public Schools, Congressman Zach Nunn, Des Moines Mayor Frank Cownie, and other public leaders in the shoot too. It dawned on me as we were wrapping up that we had gathered some of the most powerful people in the Des Moines Metro, and we were all working together on my project.

"Look around this room," I said at the end of the day. "Look at the people here—really look. Do you all understand that if we can get together, this leadership and expertise, we can change the world?" They were all taken aback. I'm not sure they had really considered the amount of power and change we had assembled for this video.

Another press conference was called to talk about the song and how we were able to gather so many influential leaders to appear in it. The message of community-building, connectedness, and real change was starting to resonate. Lt. Governor Reynolds told the press that we were friends and that she believed in my mission.

As the conference ended, I turned to Kim and asked her for her number to stay in touch. She started to give me her normal office number.

"No," I said, cutting her off. "I want your cell. We just told the press we were friends, so I want to keep in touch."

She hesitated for a second, then smiled.

"I'm going to give you this number, but don't give it to anyone," she said. I gave her my word.

A few days later, I texted her, "Hi, this is Will Keeps," just to see if she would text back. Five minutes later, she replied, and we texted back and forth for fifteen minutes.

The video dropped shortly after she became the first female governor in Iowa history. She moved into the position when then-Governor Terry Branstad became the ambassador to China. It dawned on me that I had been texting with the governor of Iowa a few short days before the announcement, and I wanted to make the most of this opportunity. I invited her to a couple of the schools I was working with so she could see what was really going on. We planned a three-school tour throughout the greater Des Moines area. At one of the schools, a couple of kids came up to her and treated her like garbage. They didn't care that Kim was the Governor or that she was trying to figure out how to help them. They treated her like any other adult that they perceived as a threat or unable to improve their situation. She was confused, as most would be, but I think it also gave her a new perspective.

I was embarrassed by this. It was my idea to do these tours, and I'd brought her into this environment. She wasn't used to being treated this way, and I wasn't sure how she would react. In the moment, my biggest fear was that I was about to lose the relationship I had worked to build with her. I couldn't shake the uneasy feeling even after the school tour had ended, so I called her to apologize. She answered right away.

"Hey, Kim. That school tour didn't go as planned, and I have a quick question for you," I said.

"Go on, Will," she replied.

"Do you trust me?" I asked.

She paused a second, then said, "Yeah."

"Okay. Then I need you trust the fact that everything that is happening is supposed to happen," I said and stopped talking.

There was another brief pause, and I could hear the smile in her voice when she said, "Okay."

We continued to build our relationship, and she opened more doors for me and Starts Right Here. She introduced me to some pretty incredible people, including US Senator Joni Ernst. Joni and I connected right away, and she got behind my dream of building the school. She even mentioned she would consider being in one of my music videos if the timing ever worked.

I started posting pictures of myself and the governor together and the things we were trying to accomplish. Doors started to open as people wondered who I was and why the governor was spending any time with me. The first major opportunity came when we were at an event together and she made eye contact with me and nodded her head in the direction of someone else in the room, Robert Cramer.

Robert is the President of Cramer and Associates, one of the largest bridge contractors in Iowa. I walked up, shook his hand, and introduced myself. We had a short conversation, and I explained that the governor had pointed him out to me. He took my information and told me he'd call to set up a lunch.

Some time went by without a call, and I ran into him again at another event with Joni Ernst. He shook my hand and mentioned that he knew he was supposed to call me, so I reminded him that he hadn't. He smiled and told me that he would change that, and he was true to his word. We found a time to grab lunch.

We covered my background, how I'd started working with kids in the Des Moines schools, and what I was working on through Starts Right Here. He listened intently, not saying too much except to ask a question here and there. The conversation ended, and he shook my hand. I wasn't able to get a good read on him, but he told me that he was going to think and pray on it, and if God wanted him to help me, he would.

God must have spoken to him because shortly after our lunch, he reached out to let me know he and his wife were going to be hosting a fundraiser for my cause. That event ended up raising $60,000 and was the spark I needed to really start generating some funding dollars. Sure, I was getting money from DHS and smaller donations here and there, but this was the single largest donation I had received, and it had come mostly from strangers. If this could happen because of the actions of a single person, I couldn't even begin to imagine what else was out there.

Kim's term was coming to an end, and her run to hold her seat as governor kicked into high gear. She announced that Adam Gregg, who had originally connected the two of us, was going to be her Lt. Governor. I called him and left a crazy-screaming voicemail at 11:30 p.m. the night of the announcement, congratulating him and wishing him luck in the upcoming election. It dawned on me that all of these people I knew were starting to move into high-profile positions, and they were endorsing me along the way. It felt like what I was doing was meant to happen and that God was working through these people to help me move Starts Right Here forward.

The campaign season was hectic and ended almost as quickly as it had started. Kim and Adam invited me to the watch party the night of the election, but I wasn't feeling the best, so I decided to stay home and watch from my couch. The numbers started to come in with the larger cities reporting first while the more rural areas lagged behind. I saw that she was falling behind her competitor, so I took a quick shower and got dressed. I remember telling my wife as I left the house that if she was going to lose, I needed to be there for her as her friend.

Chief Wingert and I almost collided at the door when I walked into the conference room where the watch party was being held.

"You must be her good luck charm, Will," he said with a huge smile on his face as he shook my hand.

"What do you mean?" I was confused, given that when I'd left the house, she been down multiple points.

Lori and Robert Cramer were standing nearby and chimed in. "As soon as you got here, Will, her numbers started to go up!"

"They're right, Will," I heard a familiar voice behind me say. It was Joni Ernst, and she was smiling, excited to see me, and the change in voting numbers.

Robert shook my hand and in front of everyone said, "You know, Will, I bet you won't go up and speak if she wins this thing." The circle now gathered around us agreed that I needed to go up there. Talk about pressure.

Joni turned to me. "I'll get you up there if you want."

"Stop playing with me," I said.

"No. It's a done deal. You're going to speak. As soon as I go up there, you follow me, and I'm going to be the one to announce you."

I started to sweat a little knowing that I was going to congratulate her in public. I thought to myself as I followed Joni, *should I faint now or later?* The next thought that crossed my mind was *who the hell do I think I am?* Why was I going on this stage, and did I even belong there? But I wanted to do this. She was my friend, and I was proud of her and what she had accomplished.

As I got up to the mic, a million thoughts raced through my mind. I wanted to say that here I stood, a Democrat in a room full of Republicans, but I do not look at you as a political party. I look at all of you as simply people. I look at myself as a person, and I voted for Kim Reynolds because I believe in her and what she's doing, not because she's a Republican. That's what I wanted to say, but there were too many cameras and lights, so instead I told everyone how proud I was of her and congratulated her on her win.

Throughout the campaign season, I had been working on the foundation for Starts Right Here. The non-profit had been created, and the papers had been filed with the government for the official

501(c)(3) status. I had recruited board members, people who believed in our cause and wanted to help see it become a reality. We found a space in downtown Des Moines that I could lease for a reasonable rate and we drew up some architectural plans to remodel the interior. We were going to have a real school with real classrooms, private study rooms, a lunch area, and the normal amenities any other school would have. But we were going to include some other things.

I knew the type of kid that would be walking through my doors. I'd been that kid growing up in Chicago. A normal school with teachers lecturing and only short breaks during every study period simply wouldn't cut it. We needed more. We needed a place for them to blow off steam when things at home weren't going well. An indoor gym would provide that release. I wanted a recording studio to show the ones interested in music that they could pursue their dreams while continuing to get their basic education. We also needed a stage and event space to showcase what these kids were doing. Most of all, we needed a porch like the one I'd grown up on. A space where we could be real and have hard conversations. A place where we could build trust and hopefully change these kids' lives forever. Starts Right Here would have all of this and more if I could raise enough money.

I started posting more on social media about our success and the relationships I was building. Selfies with Governor Reynolds were commonplace on my Facebook and LinkedIn pages. Kramer and I shared some photos after his fundraising event. It seemed like the more I posted with these influential people, the more people wanted to know who I was. I was an anomaly that caught the attention of the business community. Who was this black guy with a durag on his head who seems to be taking pictures with everyone important right now?

What I didn't expect was the blowback that started to come from Democrats and the black community. Friends and acquaintances started to look down on me for posting so many pictures with the governor and other Republicans. My inbox and social media feeds started to fill up with accusations and questions. "Why are you hanging out with them?" "Did you know what you're was doing?" "You're committing community suicide." "You're turning your back on the community, traitor." "You're just the governor's black puppet. Just her pawn."

By this point in my life, I was used to the criticism and hate. It was nothing new, and I almost expected it any time I tried to make a meaningful change. It reaffirmed that I was doing the right thing. I believed that the relationships I was building with the "other side of the aisle" were necessary to help me enrich my entire community. They could call me her pawn all they wanted because I was playing chess. If you really know how to play chess, you realize there are a lot of other pieces surrounding you, helping you to win the game. Some will fall off when the game gets too hard, and others are willing to sacrifice themselves to see you through to the end. I wanted to make it all the way across the board, because if a lowly pawn makes it there, it becomes the most powerful piece on the board—a queen. If I surrounded myself with the right pieces and made the right moves, like that pawn, I knew I could do so much more.

I wanted to be the queen so I could go where I needed to go and make the moves that were required to win the game. To my haters, it didn't matter that funding was coming in or that help was being provided to the black community. It mattered what letter was behind their name. I wanted to show them that help could come from anywhere, that it could take any form if the friendships and relationships were strong enough. The crazy part of all of this is, I'm not telling you what I wanted to happen or was hoping would happen, I'm telling you what *did* happen.

I found out that a lot of the people I was associating with and getting support from didn't understand my culture or black people.

They had seen us portrayed in the media or in movies, but they didn't have a relationship with someone who had truly lived my kind of life. As our friendships and partnerships deepened, they asked more personal questions and truly began learning what I, and countless others, had been through. It became more than just a black issue or a poverty issue or an at-risk issue. It became *their* issue. Something they now had a meaningful connection to and wanted to help solve. They wanted to see progress and believed in the steps we were starting to take.

That's why it caught me off-guard when Kim called me one afternoon and told me I needed to stop posting pictures of the two of us together.

"Why?" I demanded, wondering if I had done something wrong or had offended her.

"You're doing so much great work in the community, Will. But by posting these pictures, you're hurting yourself. People can't separate the work you're doing from the actions and bills that are being passed in the state legislature. I don't want your progress to slow down."

"Kim, you're my friend. You haven't turned your back on me, so I'm not going to turn my back on you. So, whatever you go through, I'm going to go through with you."

She thanked me and hung up. I kept getting more hate, but I'm a man of my word. I wasn't going to turn and run when things got hard. Instead, the pressure kept pushing me forward. One of my friends asked why I was doing it, why I was staying true to the governor when there was so much backlash from it.

"Because I'm willing to go through the good and bad times with her. She's given me so much support already, I'm going to walk through fire with her. We're doing this together."

"Would she do it for you?" he asked.

I thought about that question for a second. "Yeah, in my mind, I feel like she would. She is. And if it turns out that she isn't willing to, it's not going to change who I am. I'm still going to fight for what I'm doing because it's the right thing to do."

We got our bids back on the build-out for the leased space of Starts Right Here. They came in at almost exactly $500,000. The $60,000 I had received from Cramer not that long ago seemed much smaller. I was nervous and scared. How was I going to raise another $440,000 to get this funded and the program started?

I kept posting pictures of the work I was doing with Governor Reynolds and Senator Ernst all over LinkedIn and Facebook. I wanted people to see our friendship and the influence they had. It gave me more credibility and helped the fundraising. Kramer opened additional doors for me and continued to tell my story. Potential donors started to stream into the leased space to get a tour and see what we were visualizing for the future. We held an event with the governor and other prospects in the space and said a prayer at the end asking for guidance and support in making what we were doing an asset for the community. More money started to come in.

The $60,000 turned into $100,000 and then $150,000 shortly after. I gained confidence with each donation, and the $500,000 price tag didn't seem like that big of an obstacle anymore. In my mind, there was nothing in my way and no challenge I couldn't overcome. Then, March 2020 came, and despite everything I had been through and every obstacle I had overcome, I found my biggest one standing in front of me—all at once, the world simply shut down.

chapter 21

There are no words strong enough for what I felt that third week of March. In my mind, all the momentum and growth I had built up since 2017 was gone. People were scared, and I was one of them. I didn't know what to do or where to turn. My mind raced as I tried to come to terms with what was happening in the world and in my community. I debated crawling into bed and burying my head under the covers, but then who would the kids I was helping turn to? Where would they go if I gave up on them? I couldn't stop. So many things had tried to tear me down in my life, and this was just another one. I wasn't going to let Covid win. So I did what I did best—I kept fighting.

Meeting with people face-to-face didn't seem to be a reality anymore, but that didn't mean I couldn't pick up the phone and make calls or post videos giving people hope. It didn't mean I had to crawl under a rock and hide. I could still make connections, and I could still push Starts Right Here forward. If I was willing to fight, I was sure people would listen, and they did.

Money kept coming in. People saw my vision, heard my passion, and kept writing checks. They wanted to help and wanted to be a part of something big. My phone started to ring with people asking to help, asking what they could do. We hit $200,000, and almost as quickly raised $400,000. We signed contracts and started the renovation. I wanted to show people what the space would look like and provide something more concrete to demonstrate the vision I had spoken about for so many years. The build-out worked, and more people joined with their wallets and their hearts. I could see the end of the first fundraising phase in sight.

The summer of 2020 was filled with even more chaos than March. First, George Floyd was murdered in Minnesota that May. Around that same time, I posted a picture on Facebook and LinkedIn of me between Governor Reynolds and Senator Ernst congratulating the Senator on her reelection. It received some positive feedback, but far more negative. Again, I was called every name in the book and told I was turning my back on my own people and culture. But what these individuals didn't understand was that I'd done it on purpose. It was a calculated move, and it was intentional.

I wanted to show people that in spite of everything I had been through in my life, I had a voice, and I was using it to build something beautiful. By all standards, I should have been on the streets selling drugs in the best-case scenario or dead in the worst. But here I was, surrounded by some of the most influential people in the state of Iowa, and I had a seat at their table. They heard my voice, and they listened when I spoke. This was about much more than politics. It was about people coming together to make the place they live better.

Unfortunately, not many people could see that. They couldn't get past the rhetoric and hatred both sides were spewing. It told me we still had a lot of work to do, and while we were making progress, much more needed to be done.

The Black Lives Matter protests happened next, and again I was criticized for the role, or lack thereof, that I took in the marches. People wanted me in the streets, picking a side and using my voice to push an agenda. I was interrogated online and by friends and family. Why wasn't I helping them fight? Why was I standing on the sidelines when I could make a difference in what was happening right now? Didn't I believe in the cause of equality, diversity, and inclusion?

Of course I believed in BLM's message, but I didn't believe in their methods. I knew I had people around me supporting me, but I felt very much alone during that time. I had already been marching for years, but I had been marching on my own, moving the needle in my community forward one relationship at a time. I needed to keep these relationships and our mission of togetherness intact if we were going to last longer than the marches.

I decided to stick with my own personal march even though I knew it would mean a lot of fallout from the black community. My hope was that the haters would see that I was actually helping black lives through my mission. I wanted to show them that working together was so much better, and that unity could be accomplished peacefully. By working together, it's more about the community, the families, and the kids than the politics of who's right and who's wrong or the competition of who cares more.

Were people going to put a political spin on my goals? I'd be naïve to think they wouldn't, but those same people didn't see the big picture. If we let politics or disagreements halt our progress, we'd never see anything move forward.

The final piece of that summer and early fall was the enrollment of our first cohort of students into the Starts Right Here program. Construction wasn't completely finished yet, but we had classrooms, computers, and teachers who wanted to be a part of it. It may seem like a small win in the midst of the insanity of the summer of 2020, but it was the win of a lifetime in the making. Those first kids showed everyone that we had done it. We had set enough of our differences aside to let a black guy from the South Side of Chicago build a school that someone trusted enough to let their kids attend. In early 2021, our first student graduated high school.

The story doesn't stop there. During the 2021 Iowa legislative session, a bill that included my input was passed to allow easier funding for Charter Schools in the state. I wanted to help give our kids and parents an alternative to public school when they were looking for answers. The bill was, and continues to be, controversial. It wasn't about making people mad or me getting my way on additional funds from the state for Starts Right Here. It was about giving those kids and families hope. I knew from my own experience and the experiences of the kids I had worked with throughout my career, that public school simply didn't work for everyone. If we could help provide a solution that would help kids who would otherwise fail, then that's what I was going to do.

As of this book's publication date, we have led over thirty kids to graduation, each with his or her own story and motivation for walking through the doors of Starts Right Here. Some were eerily similar to how I'd grown up. Others were simply looking for hope or an alternative to a life they didn't want to live. We had some who had willingly enrolled and a couple who almost had to be dragged over the threshold. I could spend the next several pages telling stories from my perspective, but I wanted to share one in particular through the eyes of one of our kids. His name is Ala, and he was one of the kids whose life would be changed forever by Starts Right Here.

Ala was in trouble and was running out of people to turn to. He lived with his mom in Des Moines, but she was working on moving to Detroit. He had friends here, but he was set on following his mom because she was his family, and he didn't seem to have another choice. School wasn't his strong suit, and the streets had provided the support he wasn't finding at home. The Des Moines Police Department called me to reach out to him after several run-ins and close calls with the gang scene spreading through the city. I tried to call him directly, but he never picked up. I later found out that he never answered calls from numbers he didn't recognize, mostly to protect himself from additional violence or the intervention of law enforcement. So I did the next best thing and called his mom.

She picked up, and I told her who I was and that I wanted to help Ala. She told me she would help me get him on the phone, and we finally managed to talk a couple of days later. Ala was in more trouble than I'd realized. Charges had been filed against him including some involving a drive-by shooting. As we started to build a relationship, and I learned more about who he was, I realized he was a scared kid looking for help. His mom was moving, he wasn't doing well in school, and he had fallen into a bad crowd. I told him about Starts Right Here and what we were doing. He agreed to come in and see the school.

The first time Ala walked in, we hadn't finished the building. The main classroom and study rooms were complete in the front half of the building, but the porch, gym, and recording studio were still works in progress. None of that mattered to Ala. He saw my intentions and how we could help him. Shortly after the tour, he enrolled, and his mom moved to Detroit. He had some distant family in town that he moved in with, but he was basically on his own.

I had the prosecuting attorney on the drive-by case tour Starts Right Here to paint another picture of Ala than the one he had in his head. Ala had gotten it together and wanted to do better for himself. After the tour, the prosecutor was encouraged and wanted to have a meeting to go over his charges. They told him that if he was able to graduate the Starts Right Here program and stay out of trouble, they would drop the charges against him. He agreed, and we got to work.

Ala took that deal seriously and worked harder than any kid I'd ever seen. It reminded me of the time my teacher had told me my senior year of high school that I wouldn't graduate without those credits. He had something to prove and wanted to show the world that he could be somebody. I helped find him an apartment while he finished school and even found furniture so he wasn't living in an empty space. He told me he wanted to get a part-time job so he had some money. A few phone calls later, and he had one.

Ala graduated from Starts Right Here, and we found him his first-full time job. A short time later, through our connections, we got him appointed to a construction company. I keep in contact with him because I want to make sure he keeps moving forward, keeps working toward his goals and dreams, and doesn't fall back into the trap of the street.

It surprised the hell out of me when he told me he was going to have a kid and wanted to have the gender reveal party at Starts Right Here. Who would have thought so many years ago that I would be welcoming a kid I'd helped to graduate from the school I'd started to share the news of the gender of his own kid with his friends and family? On top of that, he gave me the honor of being the godfather of his kid.

I asked Ala what the program had meant for him and his future. He didn't hesitate with his response: "I'm not sure what my life would be like without you and without Starts Right Here. My life was a wreck before you called. My mom was moving, I was in trouble with the police, and everything was a mess. I don't know what would have happened. I would have been on parole or maybe in jail, but, man, that's the best case. You came at a time when there was no one else to help me, no one willing to help.

"I kept waiting for you to forget about me, you know, when you enrolled new kids or when other people became more important, but you didn't. You never forgot to call me or check in and make sure I was okay. That meant more than anything else. You didn't have to do that, but you kept on doing it, and that made me feel like someone cared."

We kept talking, and I asked him what he thought was next for him and Starts Right Here. He paused for a second before taking a breath, a smile spreading across his face. "The story ain't done yet. We're just getting started."

I've been asked many times over the last several years why I kept fighting, why I kept working toward this goal, and what motives were keeping me going. Through all the trauma, the bad home life, the molestation, the gang violence, and abuse, I could have and probably should have given up. Many times, I gave in to the monster that my upbringing had trained me to be, but beneath all of that, the real William Holmes was still there, still fighting and wanting to show up to make the world a better place.

Even after writing this book, I don't have a good answer to the question of why I'm doing this. But looking back, even though there were plenty of times I could have, and probably should have, given up, God kept pushing me through. He kept showing me the light even in the darkest of times. Without His influence in my life, I never could have overcome so much or been given the opportunities I have. I guess it comes down to this: I know it's the right thing to do. Haters are always going to be there, but many more good people are standing beside me, helping me help those who might turn out the way I should have. When I look back on my life and what I've gone through, I should still be on the street, in jail, or dead. But then, there was always some small intervention or act of God that made me realize I was here for something more; I needed to do something for someone else. So, I'm going to keep doing it. I'm going to keep working and building and showing this community that we're better off together. A small change can have a big impact, and those small changes can happen anywhere if someone is willing to take the first step. Starts Right Here has proven that, and we'll continue to prove it every day.

I think Ala said it best, "The story ain't done yet."

He's right.

It Starts Right Here.